Many A True Word

Richard Anthony Baker

headline

Cataloguing in Publication Data is available from the British Library

Hardback ISBN 978 0 7553 6515 9
Ebook ISBN 978 0 7553 6516 6

Content from Daily Telegraph house style book, page 28, © Daily Telegraph

Typeset in Bembo

Designed by James Edgar at Post98design.co.uk

Printed in Great Britain by Clays Ltd, St Ives plc

Headline's policy is to use papers that are natural, renewable and
recyclable products and made from wood grown in sustainable forests.
The logging and manufacturing processes are expected to conform
to the environmental regulations of the country of origin.

Headline Publishing Group
An Hachette UK Company
338 Euston Road
London NW1 3BH

www.headline.co.uk
www.hachette.co.uk

DEDICATED TO MY FIVE
FAVOURITE WORDS

Chorizont, someone who disputes identity of authorship, such as a person who believes Shakespeare's plays were written by Francis Bacon. [It has nothing to do with Spanish sausages. For crossword solvers, its additional attraction is that it contains the word 'horizon.]'

Gardyloo, a cry once heard from an upstairs window when the contents of a chamber pot were about to be thrown into the street

Huer, a pilchard fisherman's lookout man

Spraint, the excrement of an otter and

Zarf, a holder for a coffee cup that does not have a handle

JUST A THOUGHT

A third of all children do not have a single book of their own at home. The figure has trebled in seven years. Four out of five children believe that the Battle of Britain is a television talent show and that the Tudors are a brand of crisps. One in six teenagers leave school unable to read fluently.

CONTENTS

INTRODUCTION

My curriculum vitae says that I wrote the style book for BBC radio news. I did, but that is not the whole story. The style book of any news organisation has to be rewritten every few years to take into account changes in the use of language. So, I was one of quite a few editors. In my version, I counselled against the use of 'stand-off' in describing a siege. It was then thought to be too American, but not now. Shortly, we shall see 'battle' become a transitive verb: 'He battled cancer' [as the Americans have it] rather than 'he battled against cancer'. I opposed the transitive use, but knew I would eventually lose.

I started my career as a low-flier in BBC radio news as a member of the subs' desk responsible for Radio 4 bulletins. My fellow writers included: Lord Hall, now the Director General of the BBC and formerly the highly successful director of the Royal Opera House; Jeremy Harris, who went on to be principal adviser to two Archbishops of Canterbury; Julia Somerville, now Lady Dixon, the chairman of the committee overseeing the government's art collection; and Jennie Bond, who became the most effective of all the BBC's royal correspondents. All thoroughly nice people, I should add.

After my style book was printed, the head of news and then current affairs, Jenny Abramsky [now Dame Jennifer Abramsky], marched past me in a corridor of Broadcasting House and snorted derisorily at my support of the term 'headmaster' in preference to 'headteacher'. [She was, I am sorry to say, right.] My line manager, John Allen, surprisingly not similarly elevated, overruled my stand in favour of the split infinitive. [He was, I am sorry to say, wrong.] The brothers Fowler, Henry and Francis, the authors of *Fowler's Modern English Usage*, agree with me. [Perhaps, it would be fairer to say that I agree with them.

My admiration of them is such that I have written the libretto of a musical comedy about their lives, provisionally entitled *Say It With Fowlers*.] Those who would ban split infinitives learned Latin. In that language, it is impossible to split an infinitive because the equivalent of 'to do' or 'to make' is only one word. But we write English where a split infinitive is possible. 'To boldly go' sounds so much better than 'boldly to go' or 'to go boldly'.

My successor as style-book editor was Tom Fort, who left the BBC to write books about eels and lawns. That is to say, one book about eels, another about lawns. Incidentally, his beautiful wife, Helen, once passed on to me the best chat-up line I have ever heard. She had just returned from lunch with a similarly attractive woman. It was interrupted by a man asking 'May I buy you ladies a drink or are you too busy discussing your international modelling contracts?' What you are about to read [or discard] is largely about the English language, but, as with chat-up lines, I become distracted along the way.

Richard Anthony Baker, Leigh-on-Sea, 2013

ONE MILLION ENGLISH WORDS,
NINE MILLION GERMAN ONES

The English language is comprised of 1,022,000 words[*]. It expands by 8,500 words each year. Nearly half the new words are slang or jargon. Since 1950, the language has grown by more than 70 per cent. Over the previous 50 years, it had expanded by only 10 per cent. The addition of new words comes in waves. There was a peak in Shakespeare's time, another during the Industrial Revolution and a third now in the electronic age. People in Elizabethan England used about 150,000 words although Shakespeare's plays contain only about 18,000, some of his own making.

Most intelligent people now know about 75,000 words, 50,000 of which they use regularly. As a race, we coo or gurgle during the first three months of our lives. Between three and six months, we make vocal noises to attract attention. Between six and twelve months, we understand repeated words such as 'bye-bye'. We can speak about ten words between twelve and fifteen months. Over the following three months, that increases to twenty and we understand short sentences. By the age of two, we have about fifty words and start putting them together to ask questions[**]. Between the ages of two and three, we add another 250 words and between the ages of three and four we can make up sentences of four to six words. By the age of five, we construct well-formed sentences. By the time we reach eighteen, we recognise about 60,000 words. That is not to say they are all used. Teenagers, monitored while on the phone, were found to use 1,000 words or fewer.

[*]This compares with nine million words and compound words in German; 250,000 words in the French language, 200,000 Latin words and 100,000 Spanish ones. German compound nouns can be as long as you like. For instance, 'Donaudampfschiffahrtselektrizitätenhauptbetriebswerkbauunterbeamtengesellschaft' translates into English as the Association for Subordinate Officials of the Head Office Management of the Danube Steamboat Electrical Services, which was a subdivision of the pre-war Viennese shipping company known as Donaudampfschiffahrtsgesellschaft that transported both cargo and passengers along the Danube. [**]American researchers say parents need not worry if they stumble or say 'um' or 'er' before introducing a new word to their children. By doing so, we draw children's attention to the fact they should be on the alert for something difficult. The research was carried out at the University of Rochester in New York State. Three groups of children, aged between eighteen months and two-and-a-half years, were involved. The leading researcher was a woman called Celeste Kidd.

100 MOST-USED WORDS

1 .... the	33 .... will	65 .... good
2 .... be	34 .... my	66 ....some
3 ....to	35 .... one	67 .... could
4 ....of	36 ....all	68 ....them
5 ....and	37 .... would	69 .... see
6 .... a	38 ....there	70 ....other
7 .... in	39 .... their	71 ....than
8 .... that	40 ....so	72 ....then
9 .... have	41 ....up	73 ....now
10 I	42 ....for	74 ....look
11 .... it	43 .... out	75 ....only
12 ....for	44 ....if	76 ....come
13 .... not	45 ....about	77 .... it's
14 ....on	46 ....who	78 .... over
15 .... with	47 .... get	79 ....think
16 ....he	48 .... which	80 .... also
17 .... as	49 ....go	81 .... back
18 ....you	50 .... me	82 ....after
19 ....do	51 .... when	83 ....use
20 ....at	52 .... make	84 ....two
21 ....this	53 .... can	85 ....how
22 ....but	54 .... like	86 .... our
23 ....his	55 ....time	87 ....work
24 ....by	56 ....no	88 ....fast
25 ....from	57 ....just	89 .... well
26 ....they	58 .... him	90 .... way
27 ....we	59 ....know	91 .... even
28 ....say	60 ....take	92 .... new
29 ....her	61 .... people	93 ....want
30 ....she	62 .... into	94 ....because
31 ....or	63 .... year	95 ....any
32 ....an	64 .... your	96 ....these
		97 .... give
		98 .... day
		99 ....most
		100 .... us

Many people in this self-centred age will
be surprised that 'I' comes as low as tenth.

MISSPELLING: MEN ARE WORSE

Women are better spellers
than men. On average, they spell
86 per cent of words correctly.
For men, the figure is 83.5. People
over 50 spell, on average, 90 per
cent of words correctly. For those
under 18, the figure is 54 per cent.

WORDS MOST COMMONLY MISSPELT

accommodate; aficionado; apparatchik; until recently, barbecue would have been here as so many people spelt it 'barbeque', as in the unbearably cute 'bar-b-q'. However, lexicographers now recognise that 'barbeque' is used so frequently that it can be regarded as an alternative spelling; **broccoli; bureaucracy; calendar; chiaroscuro; connoisseur; conscience [and conscientious]; consensus; definite**

embarrass [cf. 'harass']; entrepreneur; gauge; genealogy [not geneology]; haemorrhage; harass; hierarchy; idiosyncrasy; impresario [only one 's']; indict; indispensable; inoculate

lieutenant; liquefy; littoral; manoeuvre; millennium [and millennial]; miniature; minuscule; mischievous; noticeable; occurrence [and occurred]; parallel [and parallelogram]; particular [and particularly]; pastime; perseverance; phlegm; preceding [and precedent]; prejudice; privilege; proselytise; publicity; questionnaire

restaurateur [no 'n']; rhythm*; sacrilegious; separate; supersede; unnecessary; vacillate; weird; withhold [and withheld]

... and misspell

In a *Times* spelling bee for schoolchildren, the words included coarsen, cortisone, hysteria, jodhpurs, pluperfect, rhombus and tundra. If the contest had gone on for too long, a list of extremely difficult words would have been introduced as a kind of sudden-death play-off. These included zeugma, paspalum [a type of grass] and sforzando.

---

*In the plural, it is the longest word in the English language without a vowel.

MISSPELT NAMES AND PROPER NOUNS

HANS CHRISTIAN ANDERSEN

·

BRIDGWATER, SOMERSET

·

CHISLEHURST, KENT

·

HILLARY CLINTON

·

CHARLES COBORN,
a music-hall singer

·

CHARLES COBURN,
an American actor

·

DAME JUDI DENCH

·

FLORODORA,
the musical comedy

·

BILLIE HOLIDAY,
but
MICHAEL HOLLIDAY,
Singers

·

GORDEN KAYE,
from 'Allo 'Allo

·

LETTICE AND LOVAGE,
the play

·

HUMPHREY LYTTELTON

·

LOUIS MACNEICE,
the poet

MIDDLESBROUGH

·

PAJAMA GAME,
the musical

·

RICHARD RODGERS,
the composer,
but
[LORD] RICHARD ROGERS,
the architect

·

CHIEF RABBI JONATHAN SACKS [LORD SACKS],
not 'Sachs'

·

PHILLIP SCHOFIELD,
the television presenter [with two 'l's],
but
PAUL SCOFIELD,
the actor

·

BILL SIKES,
from Oliver Twist

·

STANSTED AIRPORT

·

MOLLIE SUGDEN,
the comedy actress

·

PETE TOWNSHEND,
of The Who

·

WILFRID BRAMBELL and WILFRID HYDE-WHITE

·

THE YOUNG VISITERS,
Daisy Ashford's novel

STAGES IN THE DEVELOPMENT OF ENGLISH: FROM A SUFFOLK MEDALLION TO THE INTERNET

475
A medallion found in Suffolk provides the first evidence of written English

731
The Venerable Bede, writing in Latin, is the first person to refer to the English language

871
King Alfred, the first person to have called the language English, commissions translations from Latin into a West Saxon dialect

1066
The Norman Army, having won the Battle of Hastings, imports a language that transforms English over the next 300 years

1171
Henry II landed in Ireland, exporting English beyond Britain

End of 1300s
Chaucer writes *The Canterbury Tales*

1473
William Caxton was the first Englishman to work as a printer and the first to introduce a printing press into England

Early 1590s
Shakespeare writes his first known works, *Richard III* and the three parts of *Henry VI*

1899
Marconi sends the first radio transmissions across the English Channel

1922
The British Broadcasting Company starts transmissions from Savoy Hill, London

1989
Tim Berners-Lee invents the World Wide Web

2011
A quarter of the world's population has access to the Internet

BBC ENGLISH AND HOW SHAW
ENJOYED HIMSELF

BBC English, which was equated with the Queen's English or
Oxford English, was once described as a pronunciation of British
English based on the speech of the upper class in south-east
England. For many years that has been unfair and untrue.
During the Second World War, a Yorkshireman, Wilfred Pickles,
certainly not a member of the upper class, regularly read the news
on the Home Service, now Radio 4. Since the liberating 1960s,
all manner of regional accents have been heard. Indeed, among
some broadcasters, 'received pronunciation' is now regarded as a
negative force. The blokish Brummie, Adrian Chiles, freely admits
that his accent worked in his favour at the BBC.

At the outset, the BBC's founder, the deeply weird John Reith,
believed the company, as it was then, should set standards. In 1926,
he appointed an advisory committee on spoken English. On the
face of it, the committee, whose members included George
Bernard Shaw, the art historian Kenneth Clark and the unrivalled
broadcaster Alistair Cooke, was to decree how announcers
should pronounce contentious words. However, its secretary,
a phonetician, A. Lloyd James, had bigger ideas. He saw the
committee's remit as nothing less than 'the preservation of mutual
intelligibility throughout the English-speaking world.'

Shaw, who became its chairman in 1930, had great fun. At one
committee meeting, he insisted that 'canine' should be pronounced
'kay-nine' instead of 'car-nine', which unbelievably was then the
favoured form. 'Kay-nine,' said Shaw, was how his dentist
pronounced the word. Another member of the committee
surmised that the dentist was American. 'Of course,' said Shaw.
'Why do you think that at the age of seventy-six I still have all
my teeth?'

In 1931, the BBC published 'recommendations to announcers regarding words of doubtful pronunciation.' They prove just how much language can change even in 80 years. For instance, it was recommended that the second syllable of 'accomplish' should rhyme with 'romp'. Here are some other recommendations:

Aeroplane .... airoplayn, but the committee advises the use of the word 'airplane'

Anchovy .... the stress is on the second syllable

Chastisement .... the stress is on the first syllable

Combat .... the first syllable should be pronounced 'cum'

Culinary .... the first syllable should be pronounced 'kew'

Despicable .... the stress is on the first syllable

Harem .... hair-em

Idyll .... eye-dill

Naïve .... naa-eve

Pejorative .... pee-jor-a-tiv

Quandary .... kwon-dairy [with the stress on the second syllable]

Spontaneity .... the third syllable should rhyme with 'knee'

Tenet .... tee-net

Tryst .... pronounced as though it were 'triced'

Untoward .... unto-erd

Zebra .... zee-bra

zee-bra

kwon-dairy

In 1981, the BBC returned to the subject*. It still insisted that the third syllable of 'spontaneity' should rhyme with 'knee'. But this time, it listed the words whose mispronunciation irritated listeners most:

Comparable .... the stress should fall on the first syllable

Composite .... like 'opposite.' The last syllable should rhyme with 'sit'

Contribute .... stress on second syllable

Controversy............. stress on first syllable
Deity .... first syllable rhymes with 'see': 'dee-ity'
Dispute .... stress on second syllable
Distribute .... stress on second syllable
Government............ first 'n' fully pronounced
Jewellery .... jewel-ry, not 'joo-ler-y' [even now,
The Times spells the word 'jewelry']
Kilometre .... stress on first syllable
Primarily................. stress on first syllable
Research .... stress on second syllable
Temporarily .... stress on first syllable
[rather difficult to pronounce, though]

joo-ler-y

* This was The Spoken Word: a BBC Guide, written by Robert Burchfield, the Chief Editor of the Oxford English Dictionaries [1923–2004]. His obituary in the *Daily Telegraph* suggested he found that people's passions are easily aroused by the use of certain words in certain contexts. He was once had to appear in court to defend the right to include in the dictionary pejorative definitions of the word 'Jew', arguing that language should be treated as it is, not as some people would like it to be. He also had trouble using trade names, such as Yale locks and WeightWatchers. In addition, he kept a file of letters from readers who wanted him to coin new words, including one from a man who wanted a word for a collector of fire helmets.

British place names set many traps for foreigners, especially if visitors here believe 'cester' should be pronounced 'sester', as in Leicester [foreigners sometimes say 'Ly-sester', not, as it should be, 'Lester'] and Worcester [War-sester instead of Wooster]. East Anglia alone is full of pitfalls. Wymondham in Norfolk is pronounced 'Win-dumb', although the other Wymondham in Leicestershire is pronounced 'Why-mun-dumb'. On the north Norfolk coast, Stiffkey is 'Stookey'. Also, Happisburgh is 'Haze-bre', Godmanchester is 'Gumster', Leominster is 'Lemster', Belvoir is 'Beaver' and while Shrewsbury is pronounced 'Shroes-berry' by most people in Britain, the locals say 'Shrews-berry'.
Even the professionals get it wrong occasionally. A Radio 2 announcer referred to Aldeburgh as 'Alderberg'. It is 'Ald-bre'. Radio 2 also spoke of the Athenaeum Club as the 'A-theen-ium'. Pity also the Radio 3 announcer on his first morning introducing *The He-Brides* overture.
And, while we are about it, it is 'pronunciation', not 'pronounciation'.

Ly-sester

BRAVE NEW WORDS: FRESH DEFINITIONS

Abdicate: to give up all hope of ever having a flat stomach.

Balderdash: a rapidly receding hairline.

Circumvent: the opening in the front of boxer shorts.

Coffee: a person who is coughed upon.

Esplanade: an attempt at explanation while drunk.

Flabbergasted: appalled over how much weight you have gained.

Lymph: to walk with a lisp.

Testicle: a humorous question in an exam.

Willy-nilly: impotent.

And three suggestions from Barry Cryer, who once asked 'Who led the Pedants' Revolt?' He supplied the answer himself: 'Which Tyler.'

Asteroids: what spacemen suffer after they have sat on radiators.

Innuendo: an Italian suppository.

Oxymoron: a mad cow.

Derek Jameson once unsuccessfully sued the BBC after it was suggested that he was so ignorant he thought 'erudite' was a type of glue. He lost and it cost him a small fortune. It was typical of the BBC [then] that they employed him as a presenter so that he could earn some cash.

ENGLISH FROM FRENCH

Aperitif
A drink before a meal to stimulate the appetite. Ancient French linked the word with the equivalent of 'open' [an appetite]. So, it comes from the same source as 'aperture'.

Bric-a-brac
Knick-knacks. From *'fait de bric et de broc'*, made up of bits and pieces.

Canard
A hoax, a false report. *'Canard'* is French for duck. There is an old expression: *'Vendre un canard à moitié'*, to half-sell a duck. As that is impossible, the phrase came to mean 'to make a fool of '.

Debacle
Originally a deluge, then a stampede, now an embarrassing disaster.

Embouchure
A French word for which there is no English translation: the shape in which you should purse your lips to play a brass or woodwind instrument.

Fauteuils
Some British cinemas still have them. Theatres and trains had them once: armchairs.

Gourmand/Gourmet
Among trenchermen, a gourmand prefers quantity, a gourmet, quality. The distinction is not as great, apparently, in France.

Hors de combat
In France, literally, 'out of the fight'. In England, 'no longer able to take part'.

Insouciance
Not carelessness or indifference, but rather carefree nonchalance.

Je ne sais quoi
Literally, 'I know not what'. In other words, something indefinable.

Kir
An aperitif of dry white wine and blackcurrant liqueur. It is said to owe its popularity to the efforts of Félix Kir, a one-time Mayor of Dijon who wanted to find a way of making use of over-production of both white wine and blackcurrants round his city.

Laissez-faire
Let do. More specifically, let people do what they want to do. In Britain, the phrase is used as an adjective.

Manque
Lacking. In Britain, it is generally attached to an underachiever: he is a writer manqué. He wants to be a writer, but he isn't.

Noisette
Hazelnut in French. When applied to roast lamb, a small round piece, usually succulent.

Odalisque
A concubine in a harem and, more expansively, a ravishing, voluptuous woman.

Pierrot
A character in French pantomime, a white-faced clown. Until recently, pierrots were part of British seaside concert parties in a punning reference to seaside piers.

Queue*
In French, a tail. In English, a line of people [waiting to be served].

Roué
From '*rouer*', to break on the wheel. Roués are rakes who live only for sensual pleasure. [How wonderful!] The first were the debauched companions of the Duke of Orléans – with the suggestion that they should be punished for their behaviour.

Sabotage
To destroy on purpose. From '*saboter*' – to kick with shoes ['*sabots*'].

Tranche
At one time, a slice [of meat perhaps]. Now, an instalment, especially in financial lingo: part of a loan, a block of bonds or government stock.

Vaudeville
A variety show, which, according to some, is derived from Vau de Vire, the native valley of a Norman poet, who founded a type of convivial song. This is fanciful.

L'esprit de l'escalier
Literally means 'the wit of the staircase'. In other words, the clever riposte you think of when it is too late – the witty remark you realise you should have made while on your way out via, possibly, the staircase.

---

* Queuing is the only English word to have four consecutive vowels.

SOME WORDS AND PHRASES THAT *DAILY TELEGRAPH* JOURNOS MUST NOT USE

[at work, that is, not at home, although perhaps even there.
Who are we to look into the domestic arrangements of other people?]

Ahead of....................Before [a lazy phrase initiated by financial journalists and picked up by other hacks]

Bid.............................Attempt [headline journalism lazily transferred to the text of a story]

Crackdown................Overused

Disgraced..................Overused

Epitome of...............Overused

Fighting for his life..Trying to conquer serious illness

Gunned down...........Americanese for 'shot'

Hike..........................Meaning 'increase'

Iconic.......................Overused

Jaw-dropping...........Ridiculous attempt to lend drama to ['astounding']

Kid............................Unnecessary American abbreviation for 'child'

Local residents.........All residents are local. But why 'residents' anyway? What's wrong with 'people'?

Mass exodus.............Often silly and possibly tautologous

Nation's favourite....Who says?

Overly.......................Americanese

Probe........................Investigation [headline journalism transferred to the text of a story]

Quizzed....................What's wrong with 'questioned'?

Rubbish....................As a verb

Stretcher..................As a verb

Toilet........................Lavatory, puh-leeze

U-turn......................Since the Blessed Margaret [You turn if you want to ...], used far too frequently to denote a change of mind

CUT THE CLICHE
[an admonition mostly for hacks]

Writing for television and radio is very different from writing
for the written page. A newspaper journalist, especially one
who devises headlines, has to look for the shortest word possible
so that it fits into the smallest space allowed. But there is a danger
that journalese may then materialise, using language that people
in everyday exchanges would never countenance using.
Examples include:

Axe
As in jobs. What is wrong with 'cut'? It is still only three
letters long.

Burning issues
Are merely important ones.

Cocktail
A cocktail of drink and drugs can be made worse only when
it is lethal.

Dawn swoop
This fictitious policewoman is always present when officers
raid houses, particularly early in the morning looking for drugs,
counterfeit goods or illegal immigrants.

Genius
Shakespeare, Michelangelo and Bach were geniuses.
Clever comedians and popular singers are usually not.

Gutted
Only fish should be gutted, less so blazing buildings and,
even less than that, sportsmen.

Hell and back
People who have had a tough time all too frequently believe they have been to hell and back. Of course, they haven't.

Impeccable
Intensive research is too often impeccable.

Jammed
Switchboards sound unpleasantly messy.

Key
Useful for headlines, but not in the story itself. Try 'major' [which can also be overused] or 'important'.

Love child
Why are we still so coy in describing an illegitimate child in this way? Half of all children are now born outside marriage.

Misery
People living in poverty, with no food and incurable diseases, suffer misery. Those travelling on overcrowded trains in England do not.

Over the moon
Let us leave this locality to the jumping cow in nursery rhymes.

Princely describes princes
When attached, supposedly humorously, to a small amount of income, it merely implies lazy thinking.

Quit
To be expected in headlines, although it is only one letter fewer than 'leave' which in itself is only one letter fewer than 'resign'.

Rife

Why is speculation so frequently rife? Any of the synonyms, 'prevalent', for example, would be welcome every once in a while.

Steamy sex

I have not asked many people about this, but I have yet to hear of sex that was so torrid that it generated steam.

Topple

What happens to governments during a coup. Why not occasionally 'overthrow'?

Vigil

As in '24-hour bedside vigil'. Usually sad. But hackneyed. Try 'relatives are at the bedside'.

Waters

We must not assume that all dangerous stretches of sea are shark-infested.

LAZY LANGUAGE: SOME QUESTIONS

Why are readers so often avid? Is a beautiful speaking voice not just a beautiful voice? Has anyone heard of a dirty bill of health? Does anyone aspire to be just a pianist, rather than a concert pianist? Why is a hoax so frequently elaborate? Why do we talk about free gifts? Aren't gifts always free? What is rude about good health? Shall we banish light entertainment until someone invents heavy entertainment? Need an old age be ripe? Are you allowed to be a recluse or must you always be something of a recluse? Are campaigners always tireless? Is it possible to be unaware without experiencing bliss? May we talk about obscurity rather than virtual obscurity? And will you allow me to be inadequate rather than woefully inadequate?

MISLEADING INFORMATION

The *New Statesman* once set as the subject of a competition:
Misleading Information for Tourists Visiting London.
Among the entries:

ON ENTERING AN UNDERGROUND
TRAIN, IT IS CUSTOMARY TO SHAKE
HANDS WITH EVERY PASSENGER.

·

THE YELLOW LINES AT ROADSIDES
INDICATE THE NUMBER OF ROWS
OF CARS THAT ARE ALLOWED TO
PARK THERE.

·

And a cruel one for children:

A TUNE PLAYED BY AN ICE-CREAM
VAN INDICATES THAT SUPPLIES HAVE
JUST RUN OUT.

'MY POSTILLION HAS BEEN STRUCK ...

... by lightning' is often quoted as the best example of the most useless sayings contained in foreign phrase books. A postillion [or postilion], incidentally, is a man who rides a horse drawing a coach. A coachman, by contrast, travels on the coach itself alongside the passengers. At Trooping the Colour [not, it should be pointed out, Trooping of the Colour], the Queen has a postillion. Dirk Bogarde entitled the first volume of his autobiography *A Postillion Struck by Lightning* because, on holiday as a child, he found an old phrase book using the saying. *Punch* magazine [30 August 1916] contains the line 'An officer serving in the Balkans writes to say that he has just come across a Hungarian/English phrase book which starts with the sentence "My postillion has been struck by lightning."' The 1877 edition of a John Murray guide contains translations of 'Oh dear, the postillion has been thrown off. Is he hurt? Run for assistance to the nearest cottage.' Earlier, Baedeker's phrase book [1870] gives German, French and Italian translations of 'Are the postillions insolent?'

Other phrase books have equally odd examples 'Are you fond of bagpipes?'; 'When do huckleberries get ripe?'; 'Is it OK if I bring my laptop in the sauna?'; 'The women will dance delicately round the tree'; 'My milkman is dishonest'; 'Could you please send for the hall porter? There appears to be a frog in my bidet'; and 'My aunt hates cheese, but she plays the saxophone quite well'. [Why is the conjunction a 'but'?]

It is often as hard to discover the provenance of these sayings as it is to find out when a joke was first cracked. The line Talbot Rothwell gave to Kenneth Williams in *Carry on Cleo* [1964], 'Infamy! Infamy! They've all got it in for me', was 'borrowed' from the radio show *Take It From Here* [1948-60], in which Frank Muir and Denis Norden wrote the joke for Dick Bentley when, as Caesar, he was attacked by Brutus.

An on-line experiment was carried out among 300,000 people around the world to try to find the funniest joke ever. This was the winner:

> Two hunters are out in the woods of New
> Jersey when one of them collapses. He appears
> to have stopped breathing and his eyes are
> glazed. His friend immediately reaches for
> his mobile and calls the emergency services.
> He tells them: *'I think my friend has died.*
> *What can I do?'* The operator says: *'Take it easy.*
> *I can help. First, let's make sure he is dead.'*
> There is a silence and then a shot is heard.
> The hunter gets back on the phone and says:
> *'OK. Now what?'*

That joke was heard fifty years earlier in a television sketch written by Spike Milligan for Peter Sellers and Michael Bentine and set far away from New Jersey.

Hecklers are still a problem for comedians. They abound in comedy clubs and most of the putdowns delivered by the comics are absolutely filthy.

Two [clean] rejoinders I have enjoyed:
From Arthur Smith:
'Do I hear the long-term side effects of Junior Aspirin?'

And from Jo Brand:
'Where's your girlfriend? Out grazing, I presume.'

But all these people are mere beginners when compared with the great Ken Dodd, who said: *'I knew the Falklands War was about to start when I passed Vera Lynn's house and heard her gargling.'*

WAYS TO INSULT MEN OF LOW IQ

HE'S A FEW SANDWICHES SHORT OF A PICNIC.

·

HIS LIFT DOESN'T GO ALL THE WAY TO THE
TOP FLOOR.

·

THE LIGHTS ARE ON, BUT NO ONE'S AT HOME.

·

HE'S DEPRIVING SOME VILLAGE OF ITS IDIOT.

·

HIS RECEIVER'S OFF THE HOOK.

·

IF YOU GAVE HIM A PENNY FOR HIS THOUGHTS,
YOU'D GET CHANGE.

·

HE DOESN'T HAVE ALL HIS OARS IN THE WATER.

·

And from Australia:

THE WHEEL IS TURNING, BUT THE HAMSTER IS DEAD.

APHORISMS

A. P. Herbert *[1890-1971]* was a rum cove. He was a novelist, humorist, parliamentarian and an activist for law reform. If he is remembered for anything, it is for the lyrics of 'This is My Lovely Day', which he wrote to Vivian Ellis's melody for *Bless the Bride* [1947]. [Come to think of it, he is probably not even remembered for that.]

He was also a fierce observer of the way in which the English language changed. In 1935, he wrote a book called *What a Word!* It is instructive to note what exercised him then. The word 'eventuality' had evidently just become commonplace:

> *We make an adjective out of 'event' — 'eventual'*
> *and some hog adds an 'ity' to the adjective and the*
> *solemn lexicographer welcomes the reptile into his*
> *book. These words increase like duckweed or the lower*
> *forms of animal life. I wonder that 'eventualitarian'*
> *has not yet emerged from the warm swamps in which*
> *the slug-words are born.*

You can see what he means. I cringed when I first heard the word 'vandalise' in the 1960s. It means no more than 'damage', I thought. But it does. It means 'damage by vandals'. It is almost the same as 'hospitalise', which still sounds ugly. I would rather use the three words 'take to hospital' than the one. [While we're about it, let's abolish the journalist's 'rushed to hospital'. As far as I know, no one has ever been taken to hospital slowly. And people are not released from hospital. They are discharged. Hospitals are not prisons. Also, have you noticed that, while the rest of us are merely taken ill, actors always collapse?]

APH hated 'television' too: 'a monster, half Latin ["visio" from "*videre*"] ["see"], half Greek ["*tele*" meaning "far"]'. But it is only a monster to people who know it is a hybrid. Was APH similarly critical of automobile, bigamy, dysfunction, electrocution, hyperactive, liposuction, nonagon, quadraphonic and sociology? He also rampaged against the style of office letters written in 1935 and showed how they could be phrased more succinctly:

> *We are in receipt of your favour of the 9th inst. with regard to the estimate required for the removal of your furniture and effects from the above address to Burbleton and will arrange for a representative to call to make an inspection on Tuesday next the 14th inst. before 12 noon which we trust will be convenient after which our quotation will at once issue.*

This is one sentence of 66 words. APH showed how it could be cut by a third.

> *We have your letter of May 9 requesting an estimate for the removal of your furniture and effects to Burbleton and a man will call to see them next Tuesday morning, if convenient, after which we will send the estimate without delay.*

Forty-two words, but still one sentence.

Although able to speak perfectly good English conversationally, some people writing business letters adopt peculiarly stilted language.

APH provided a quick translation of terms and phrases found in official letters:

Advise .... Tell, inform
Appreciate .... Understand, realise
A substantial percentage [or proportion] .... Some, much
Communicate .... Write
Furnish particulars .... Give details

Institute the necessary inquiries .... Make inquiries
It will be our endeavour .... We shall try
Our representative .... A man
The same .... It
We are at present desirous .... We wish
We are in agreement .... We agree
We are in receipt of .... We received
We are of the opinion .... We think
We beg to acknowledge .... We thank you
Your further favour .... Your second letter
Your good selves .... You —— swine

GOBBLEDYGOOK

Such letters as those quoted by A. P. Herbert are no longer
written, but, forgetting their verbose old-world courtesies,
they could at least be understood. Today, a corporate distortion
of the language threatens to destroy at least a part of it. Its main
aim is that, by employing jargon and gobbledygook, it renders
comprehension of the language less easy. It lies and it obfuscates.
George Orwell foresaw the tendency in his novel, *1984*. Writing
in 1948, Orwell introduced the word 'newspeak', an attempt by
the authorities to influence thought by the manipulation of
language. In 'Politics and the English Language', Orwell wrote:

> *A man may take to drink because he feels himself
> to be a failure and then fails all the more completely
> because he drinks. It is rather the same thing that is
> happening to the English language. It becomes ugly
> and inaccurate not because our thoughts are foolish,
> but the slovenliness of our language makes it easier
> for us to have foolish thoughts.*

The acclaimed textbook on good English, *The Complete Plain Words*, rules that jargon used purely within a profession is pardonable. In newspaper journalism, for instance, a slug is the title of a story. If the story runs for 24 hours or so, adding facts and changing emphases, it becomes a running slug. Journalists using jargon like this between themselves understand what they are talking about. It would be ridiculous if they spoke in such a way to anyone outside the profession. *The Comlete Plain Words* quotes an imaginary example of jargon:

> *These are all time-expired clause 4 optants and delay in word referral would distort the quarterly submission-ratio. If the claimant is ineligible for transitional supplement only because he has no dormant assets, the initiating officer should consider extra-statutory disregard.*

It is an ugly piece of English, but it efficiently does what it sets out to do. Both writer and reader understand its meaning. To rephrase the passage in a form intelligible to the uninitiated would take at least five times the space and make it possibly less clear to the initiated.

The Italian-Jewish writer, Primo Levi, was more concerned with what he called public language that defies normal understanding. It was, he wrote, 'an ancient repressive artifice known to all churches, the typical vice of our political class (and) the foundation of all colonial empires.'

Don Watson quotes Levi in his splendid book, *Gobbledygook*. He turns to the International Federation of Journalists and its code of conduct, which states that the first duty of the journalist is respect for the truth and the right of the public to truth. Watson adds: 'There can be no respect for the truth without respect for the language. Only when language is alive does truth have a chance.'

Yet, during the war against Iraq, many media representatives accepted the language of military officers without question. When the military reported that 70 per cent of a group of Iraqi soldiers had been 'degraded', some journalists did not bother to change the word to 'killed'. Indeed, one newsman accepted 'pureed' as a synonym for 'killed'.

In corporate and government language, watch out for the following [and they are only starters]:

Architect [as a verb]
A useless addition to the language. 'Build' or 'design' are perfectly adequate.

Blue-sky thinking
Dreaming up new ideas. Compare with the clear blue water that has to exist between political parties to show they have different policies. 'Boris [Johnson] has recently been putting lots of clear blue water between him and the Cameron government and the Tory grass roots clearly like what they see.'

Core competencies
The essential part of an individual's job. That's all.

Disincentive
An ugly word discouraging someone or something.

Empower
To empower people is merely to give them the authority or make them feel able to do something. It need not sound so all-important.

Functionality
Merely the capacity something has to be practical.

Gardening leave
Enjoyed by someone sent home on full pay without having to do any work. It can apply to someone whom employers dare not sack in case he or she sues them.

Headcount reduction
A loss of jobs.

Impactful
The creation of an adjective from 'impact' is supposed to show greater importance.

Joined up
Used to describe governments with ministries that know what each other is doing.

Key driver
Ridiculous phrase for 'important stimulus', usually economical.

Liquidity shortfall
Preposterous synonym for 'lack of cash'.

Misspeak
If you say something you regret, you can claim you misspoke. After Hillary Clinton had visited Bosnia in 1996, she said that her plane had landed under fire and that she had to run to her vehicle. But television footage showed her disembarking normally and strolling across the tarmac. Mrs Clinton said she had misspoken: what you and I would call lying.

Neutralise
In times of war, 'kill'. Another euphemism.

Outsourcing
Originally, subcontracting. Now used when companies sack staff and use occasional freelancers to take their place.

Pre-plan
What does 'pre-plan' have that 'plan' hasn't? A plan will always be something that has to be done in advance, so the shorter word is always preferable.

Quantitative easing
Whichever way you look at it, printing new money.

Quantum leap
Borrowed from physics, a spectacular advance. Usually gross exaggeration.

Road map
Merely a plan showing the way forward.

Sea change
Originally, a complete transformation akin to the gravitational force of global tides. Now, a change of just about anything.

Transparency
It once meant being able to see through something. The revisionists would have us believe that it now means being completely honest.

Uptick
A trendy word for 'increase'.

Vision
A grander word than 'plan' or 'hope'. Politicians are judged by whether they have 'the vision thing'.

Win-win
A deal which no one can lose. Impossible, of course. There is always a loser. That is why 'a no-win situation' is heard more frequently.

THE GOOD BOOK

On the 400th anniversary of the King James Bible, the Bible Society in England and Wales and the Scottish Bible Society released the results of a survey showing that many people fail to realise how many everyday phrases come from the Good Book. More than half knew that Cain used the expression 'my brother's keeper' after he had murdered Abel. But nearly a quarter attributed 'filthy lucre' to Shakespeare rather than the Book of Timothy. 'Writing's on the Wall' was a track on a George Harrison album, but it was recorded 370 years after 'the writing on the wall' appeared in the Book of Daniel. Here are some phrases first used in the Bible:

All things to all men .... *1 Corinthians 9.22*
'*To the weak became I as weak that I might gain the weak. I am made all things to all men that I might by all means save some.*' It is hard to know what Paul is going on about here. He appears to be saying 'I display different attitudes to different people so that I can please everyone', not the most exemplary behaviour.

Cast thy bread upon the waters ....*Ecclesiastes 11.1*
Cast thy bread upon the waters for thou shalt find it after many days.
You can read this in one of two ways:
1. if you send ships selling grain to many different ports, some are bound to be admitted *or*
2. if you cast seeds on shallow water, some will take root.
   The lesson is that a distribution of your assets will [or should] eventually yield returns.

Death, where is thy sting? .... *1 Corinthians 15.55*
Eat, drink and be merry..*Luke 12.19*
[Be] fruitful and multiply..................................... *Genesis 1.22*
How are the mighty fallen .... *2 Samuel 1.19*
In the twinkling of an eye......................... *1 Corinthians 15.52*
Judge not..*John 7.24*

Kick against the pricks ....*Acts 9.5*
It is hard for thee to kick against the pricks. [Stop sniggering in the
back pews.] Pricks were sticks with pointed spikes at one end.
Agricultural labourers working with oxen often jabbed the cattle
with the sticks in a way that made them work harder. If the cattle
refused, the spikes dug deeper into their flesh. Possible moral:
don't bother to retaliate. It'll only get worse.

Let us now praise famous men........................*Ecclesiastes 44.1*

Many are called, but few are chosen............... *Matthew 22.14*
[As those who have attended countless auditions and
appointments boards will testify.]

No new thing under the sun...............................*Ecclesiastes 1.9*
Out of the mouths of babes.............*Psalms 8.2 Matthew 21.16*
Powers that be .... *Romans 13.1*
Root of the matter..*Job 19.28*
Still small voice ....*1 Kings 19.12*
Thorn in the flesh .... *2 Corinthians 12.7*
Unclean, unclean ....*Leviticus 13.45*
Vanity of vanities...*Ecclesiastes 1.2*
Woe is me... *Psalms 120.5*

Ye cannot serve God and Mammon .... *Matthew 6.24*
Mammon encapsulates greed and excessive materialism. With a
capital 'm', it signifies a false god of riches.

SOUNDBITES

Usage of the definite or indefinite article can make all the difference. It is obviously 'the actor, Sir Kenneth Branagh', but someone in rep in Wigan is probably 'an actor'. So at what point does 'an actor' become 'the actor'? Also: why in restaurants do we place an order for, say, 'the trout'? 'I'll have the trout please.' We know the kitchens are bound to have more than one trout.

Which language is Häagen Dazs, the yummy ice cream taken from? No language. The word was made up to sound Scandinavian. One of the founders of the ice cream, Reuben Mattus, a Polish Jew living in New York, sat at his kitchen table for hours saying nonsensical words until he came up with a combination he liked.

If you reiterate something, you are iterating it. 'Iterate' means repeat. A quag is a bog. A mire is a bog. And so is a quagmire. To zag is to zigzag. To zig is to zigzag. So, 'zigzag' is really redundant.

Why does the lady making the recorded announcement at the end of a rail journey say 'Please remember to take all your belongings with you when you leave the train'? She must know that nearly all our belongings are at home. We have brought only a few with us.

An eavesdropping: two women talking on a bus about a male acquaintance:
'*You know he's been in hospital.*'
'*Mmm.*'
'*Of course, it'll never be of any use to him again. Not as a leg.*'

TOO CLOSE FOR COMFORT

Some rules never sink in. Every time I use the word 'draft' as in 'draft plan', I have to look it up, nagged that I should be spelling it 'draught'. An explanation of similar twosomes may prevent you from becoming Mrs Malaprop's natural heir:

Affect/Effect
For the most part, 'affect' is a verb meaning to cause something to happen. 'Effect' is a noun meaning 'result'.

Amoral/Immoral
If you are amoral, you don't recognise the difference between right and wrong. If you are immoral, you know what morals are, but you deliberately choose to ignore them.

Apiary/Aviary
Bees are kept in apiaries, birds in aviaries.

Arouse/Rouse
To arouse is to stimulate. To rouse is to stir up.

Astrology/Astronomy
Astrology is concerned with the presumed influence of stars and planets over people and events. [Horoscopes and all that.] Astronomy is the rather more serious study of stars and planets. [Sir Patrick Moore and all that.]

Biannual/Biennial
Biannual events happen twice a year, biennial ones every two years.

Boarder/Border
A boarder attends a boarding school. A border is a boundary [between two countries, for instance].

Canon/Cannon

A canon is an ecclesiastical law or a comprehensive list of an author's or musician's works. A cannon is a gun.

Complement/Compliment

A complement is the number or quantity required to make something complete. A compliment is an expression of praise.

Continual/Continuous

Continual describes something that happens again and again. Continuous describes something that happens without stopping.

Covert/Covet

'Covert' is the opposite of 'overt'; so, 'concealed'. 'Covet' is a verb meaning 'to wish for', usually involving something that belongs to someone else.

Dhaka/Dakar

Dhaka is the capital of Bangladesh. Dakar is the capital of Senegal.

Discreet/Discrete

A discreet person keeps secrets. Discrete means distinct: 'We divided the work into discrete sections.'

Draft/Draught

A draft plan is a preliminary one. A draught can blow under a door.

Dual/Duel

'Dual' describes something doubled, like a carriageway.
A duel is a fight between two people that often ends up messily.

Erotica/Exotica

Erotica is [are?] usually a polite synonym for pornography.
Exotica comes from a beautiful faraway foreign land.

Firing line/Line of fire

If you are in the firing line, you are not in danger. The firing line is made up of men with guns trained on someone who is about to be killed. That person is in danger. He is in the line of fire.

Flair/Flare

A flair is a natural aptitude. 'To flare' is 'to erupt in anger'.

Flaunt/Flout

If you flaunt, you show off. If you flout, you ignore.

Flounder/Founder

'To flounder' is to get into difficulties. 'To founder' is to sink.*

Glebe/Grebe

'Glebe' is church land. A grebe is a seabird.

Grenada/Granada

Grenada is a Caribbean country. Granada is the capital city of the province of Granada in the autonomous community of Andalusia in Spain.

Groin/Groyne

Groin is your sexual tackle. A groyne is a breakwater separating beaches.

Gunboat/Gunship

A gunboat, as you might expect, is a boat armed with guns while a gunship, oddly enough, is an aircraft equipped for ground attack missions.

Hangar/Hanger

A hangar for aircraft. A hanger for clothes. [For low hangers, look elsewhere.]

---

*An early-morning Radio 2 bulletin edited by a journalist who has written a book laying down laws about language referred to the *QE2* foundering. After several phone calls from old salts, I [that is to say, the journalist] looked the word up in a dictionary.

Hoard/Horde
A hoard is a cache of treasures. A horde is a crowd.

Ibex/Ilex
An ibex is a mountain goat. Ilex is holly.

Intense/Intensive
'Intense' is 'extreme' or 'deep'. 'Intensive' is forcing many tasks, perhaps, into a short space of time.

Invaluable/Unvaluable
Something invaluable has such a high value that it cannot be valued. Something unvaluable is worthless.

Militate/Mitigate
To militate is to help to prevent. To mitigate is to alleviate.

Onyx/Oryx
An onyx is a gem. An oryx is an antelope.

Ordnance/Ordinance
Ordnance is artillery. Ordinance is a decree.

Oregano/Origami
Oregano is a herb. Origami is the art of paper folding.

Overestimate/Underestimate
When Chris Evans left BBC Radio 1, its controller, Matthew Bannister, said: 'His contribution cannot be underestimated.' What did he mean?

Paramount/Tantamount
'Paramount' is 'most important'. 'Tantamount' is 'equal'.

Precede/Proceed

'Precede' is 'come before'. 'Proceed' is 'go ahead'.

Prostate/Prostrate

[Very commonly misconstrued.] A prostate is a gland.
Prostate cancer is the second biggest killer of men amongst
cancers. When you are prostrate, you are lying down.

Quash/Squash

You quash a rumour. You squash something by perhaps sitting
on it heavily.

Regime/Regimen

A regime is a system of government, often used pejoratively.
A regimen is a course of treatment.

Regrettable/Regretful

Regrettable applies to incidents or situations. It means causing or
deserving regret. Regretful refers to people who are full of regret.

Serf/Surf

A serf is a slave. 'Surf' is 'surging tide' or as a verb 'to search
the Internet'.

Sewage/Sewerage

Sewage is waste matter that runs through pipes. These pipes
are sewerage.

Stalactite/Stalagmite

A stalactite hangs from the roof of a cave. A stalagmite grows
from its floor. There is a mnemonic. Stalactite has a 'c' in it;
stalagmite a 'g'. 'C' equals ceiling. 'G' equals ground.

Stationary/Stationery
Stationary is static. Stationery is notepaper.

Suede/Swede
Suede is a type of leather. A Swede is a native of Sweden.
A swede is a turnip.

Summon/Summons
To summon is to call someone to appear. To summons is to call
someone to appear in court.

Titillate/Titivate
To titillate is to excite. To titivate is to make someone or
something look his/her/its best.

Tortuous/Torturous
If you are tortuous, you are devious. If you are torturous,
you cause violent distortions.

Troop/Troupe
A troop consists of soldiers; a troupe, entertainers.

Uninterested/Disinterested
Uninterested means not showing any interest. Disinterested
means impartial.

Venal/Venial
Venal means corruptible. In theology, a venial sin is far less serious
than a mortal one.

Wrest/Wrestle
To wrest is to seize by force. To wrestle is to strive to overcome.

AN AMERICAN VIEW OF EUROPE

The British, who are feeling the pinch after recent terrorist
threats, have raised their security level from 'miffed' to 'peeved'.
Soon, though, security levels may be raised yet again to 'irritated'
or even 'a bit cross'. Londoners have not been 'a bit cross' since
the Blitz in 1940 when tea supplies all but ran out. Terrorists
have been re-categorised from 'tiresome' to 'a bloody nuisance'.
The last time the British issued 'a bloody nuisance' warning level
was during the Great Fire of 1666.

The French government announced that it had raised its terror
alert from 'run' to 'hide'. The only two higher levels in France are
'surrender' and 'collaborate'. The rise was precipitated by
a recent fire that destroyed France's white flag factory, in effect,
paralysing the country's entire military capability.

It is not only the English and the French who are on a heightened
level of alert. Italy has increased its alert level from 'shout loudly
and excitedly' to 'elaborate military posturing'. Two higher
levels remain: 'ineffective combat operations' and 'change sides'.
The Germans also increased their terror alert from 'disdainful
arrogance' to 'dress in uniform and sing marching songs'.
They also have two higher levels: 'invade a neighbour' and 'lose'.

Belgians, on the other hand, are all on holiday, as usual, and the
only threat they are worried about is NATO pulling out of
Brussels. The Spanish are excited to see their new submarines
ready to deploy. These beautifully designed subs have glass
bottoms. So, when sailing round Britain, the new Spanish Navy
can get a really good look at the old Spanish Navy.

HOW TO SOLVE FIENDISH CROSSWORDS
[with thanks to the compilers of puzzles in **The Times,** *the* **Daily Telegraph** *and the* **Independent***]*

Many people who enjoy 'quick' crosswords look at their cryptic counterparts and are immediately lost. The usual cry is 'Even when I know the answer, I don't know how it's arrived at'. Compilers of cryptic crosswords do not set out to try to beat you into submission, however difficult the puzzle may seem. Their aim is to engage you in a contest of verbal agility, which you may or may not win. The setter tries to fool you. He [and there are precious few women compilers; women probably have better things to do] wants to trick you into thinking about one subject, when really the clue is about another. A *Daily Telegraph* clue, 'Following Arbuckle's lead, the metamorphosis of Chaplin, a true star [5, 8]' would have you believe that this is all about Fatty Arbuckle, Charlie Chaplin and the silent film era. It is, in fact, about astronomy. 'Arbuckle's lead' is merely his first letter, 'a'. The metamorphosis, in other words, an anagram of 'Chaplin, a true' leads to 'Alpha Centauri', the third brightest star in the sky and the closest to the sun.

Anagrams

When I was at secondary school, I spent more time trying to solve crosswords than studying English. So, at the end of two years, T. S. Eliot was to me no more than an anagram of 'toilets' and surprisingly 'litotes'. Here is a real clue: 'Misguided love is pity really [10]'. 'Misguided' indicates that an anagram is on the way. 'Love is pity' make ten letters. So, the answer is 'positively' meaning 'really'.

There is a complex variety of words indicating that you should have to make anagrams of words in a clue. They include: amiss, anyhow, arrange, bananas [and all words representing madness], break, burst, comic, complicate, doctor [as a verb], drunk [and all its synonyms], eccentric, esoteric, fantastic, hammer [as a verb], hit, implicate, improve, in error, lost, mess, mobile, muddle, odd, organise, out of place, possibly, reassemble, resort, revise, run, shift, smash, somehow, sort, tangle, transmutational, treat, upset, wimpy, work and many more. In fact, the newest edition of *Chambers Dictionary* lists 759 words that indicate anagrams.

Hidden solutions

The answer is to be found in the body of the clue. 'One who believes in British industry [5]'. 'In' is the word alerting you to a hidden solution. 'British industry' conceals 'Hindu', one who believes. And there are reversed hidden solutions: 'Puts down a bit of unease to medicine being upped [7]'. 'A bit of' indicates a hidden solution, but this time the solution is to be found in reverse. 'Unease to medicine' contains 'demotes' in reverse ['upped']. Demotes = puts down.

Homophones

Words that sound alike have their part in crossword clues. 'Sentence like wordplay, might you say? [6]'. The answer is 'punish', a criminal sentence, which sounds like 'punnish', 'relating to wordplay'.

Initials

Be on your guard for clues whose solutions are made up of initial letters. 'Bad emotional experience foolishly starts quarrel [4]'. The initial letters [starts] of 'bad emotional experience foolishly' spell 'beef', a synonym for 'quarrel'.

Every other letter

Some clues can be answered only by looking at alternate letters. 'Remove all traces of fear with batsmen? The odds are non-existent [5]'. The second sentence indicates there is a word or words in the first sentence that must lose every other letter. Alternate letters in 'fear' are 'e' and 'r'. Every other letter of 'batsmen' spell out 'a', 's' and 'e'. Together, they make 'erase', 'remove all traces'.

All-in-one clues

So called because both wordplay and definition are fused to give you the answer. 'This is for shielding face [5]'. Answer: 'vizor'. 'Viz' equals 'This is'. 'For shielding face' is 'for' without its 'face', the letter 'f'. 'Viz' and 'or' = vizor, which shields your face. More simply, 'Worship a god appropriately within [6]' is a 'hidden' clue, but also works as an 'all in one'. The answer is 'pagoda'.

Letter switch clues

'Chefs have names for cold corners [5]'. Chefs are cooks. 'Names for cold' signifies that the letter 'n' should replace the letter 'c'. Therefore, nooks [corners] is the answer.

Synonyms

Straightforward multiple definitions. 'Fight a spell of illness [4]'. 'Bout' is both 'part of a fight' and 'a period of illness'.

Words within words

One word inserted in another. 'It's done in fish collector [8]'. 'It's done' as an exclamation that equates with 'there'. 'Gar' or 'garpike' is an American freshwater fish. 'There' in 'gar' = gatherer, a collector. Words within words are often indicated by the verb, 'pen'. The solution for 'examine page penned by six-footer' is 'inspect': 'page', the letter 'p', penned [kept in] by an insect [a creature, usually, with six feet]. 'Examine' = 'inspect'. In this context, 'bear' and 'store' are synonyms of 'pen'.

Most cryptic clues are made up of elements of all the above categories and other devices designed to trip you up. For instance, 'Writer's profession lacking new hip art's development [13]'. 'Calling' equates with 'profession', but lacking 'new', 'n', makes it 'callig'. 'Development' signifies an anagram of 'hip art's' ['raphist']. 'Callig' plus 'raphist' equal calligraphist, a writer.

To complete a cryptic crossword, you will need to have mastered ordinary abbreviations, those of foreign countries and American states and other bits and pieces.

ABBREVIATIONS
From 'about, c, ca [circa] and re [office language: "about the matter"]' through to 'Zero, o'.

American states
The abbreviations of American states, as recognised by the United States Postal Service, constitute an essential tool for compilers: from Alabama, AL, through to Wyoming, WY.

Chemical elements
Keep a list of abbreviated elements close at hand, particularly: ag, silver; as, arsenic; au, gold; cu, copper; fe, iron; ni, nickel; pb, lead, which has the benefit of being pronounced in two ways; sn, tin.

Compass points
It is not hard to remember N [north], S [south], E [east] and W [west] and some of the bits in between. A compass point can be indicated by the word 'point' or 'quarter'.

Countries
There are recognised abbreviations of foreign countries from Afghanistan, AF, to Zimbabwe, ZW.

Cricket
A minimal knowledge of cricket is required, enough to equate deliveries with an over and that an extra is a bye and that 'leg' can be 'on' and batting 'in'. [From tennis, compilers occasionally borrow 'love' to indicate nothing or the letter 'o'.]

Currency
A glancing acquaintanceship with the currencies of some foreign countries is also useful, most notably:

Albania, lek; Azerbaijan and Turkmenistan, manat; Bangladesh, taka; Botswana, pula; Cambodia, riel; Croatia, kuna; Ethiopia, birr; Georgia, lari; Ghana, cedi; Haiti, gourde; Hungary, forint; Kazakhstan, tenge. North and South Korea, won; Kyrgyzstan, som; Laos, kip; Latvia, lats; Lesotho, loti; Lithuania, litas; Macau, pataca; Myanmar, kyat; Papua New Guinea, kina. Romania, leu; Thailand, baht; Uzbekistan, som; Vanuatu, vatu; Vietnam, dong; Western Somoa, tala.

Foreign languages
Some knowledge of other European languages is useful, such as the definite and indefinite articles in French and German. A smattering of further French can come in handy, enough to know, for instance, that 'nous' is the French for 'we' and that 'été' is 'summer'. Letters of the Greek alphabet should be learned, most importantly alpha, beta, eta, mu, nu, xi, pi, rho, tau, phi, chi and psi.

NATO's phonetic alphabet of words can be pronounced and understood clearly in radio and telephone messages. So, it is useful for compilers searching for an unusual way to indicate one letter: Alpha, Bravo, Charlie, Delta, Echo, Foxtrot, Golf, Hotel, India, Juliet, Kilo, Lima, Mike, November, Oscar, Papa, Quebec, Romeo, Sierra, Tango, Uniform, Victor, Whisky, X-ray, Yankee, Zulu.

Roman numerals
one, i; four, iv; five, v; six, vi; nine, ix; ten, x; 40, xl; 50, l; 60, lx; 90, xc; 100, c; 400, cd; 500, d; 600, dc; 900, cm; 1,000, m.

Crossword words
Only in a crossword will you find an aileron, a flap in an aircraft wing; an étui, a needle-case; the edible mollusc known as an abalone; and a narwhal, a whale. Surprisingly, two other whales, an orc and an orca, often bask in crosswords. The fencing sword known as the épée appears more regularly than it would in everyday conversation. The Inca, members of a one-time Peruvian

civilisation, and the Impi, a Zulu regiment, crop up with startling frequency. As do the Ides, the thirteenth day of the month in the Latin year, but the fifteenth in March, May, July and October. The Ides can be fateful as they were on that day in March 44 BC when Caesar was killed.

Because of the need to keep the component parts of an answer short, a drug in a clue is often E, ecstasy; a port, Rio; a priest, Eli, one of the last judges before the rule of kings commanded ancient Israel; a town, Diss [Norfolk]; a river, the Po [in northern Italy], the Dee or the Exe; an old city, Ur, once on the Iraqi coast near the mouth of the Euphrates on the Persian Gulf. A Scot is usually 'Ian'. A drink can be 'it', as in a gin and it [Italian sweet vermouth]. 'One' can be a joke, as in 'Have you heard the one about...?' A see can be the seat in a bishop's diocese where his cathedral is situated. Ely in Cambridgeshire is favoured in crosswords. A support is often a bra, a tee or an easel. A flower, pronounced to rhyme with 'lower', is a river. Also banker, an Australian word denoting a river that is on the point of overflowing. Neat can be cattle, such as an ox. A party is always a 'do'. And any fuss is 'ado'. 'Races' may be 'TT'. 'Regret' is always 'rue'. 'Vessel' is a wretched word in clues. It can refer to a sailing vessel or a kitchen utensil – and there are dozens of those.

You will find the occasional reference to changing sides. That means changing right ['r'] for left ['l'] and vice versa. So, that 'room' could become 'loom' and 'lace' could become 'race'. Great wordplay can be made of words associated with marriage. 'Intended' can be 'fiancé' [and 'fiancée'] and a marriage itself is often a 'match' or a 'union'.

Once you have mastered all that, cryptic crosswords are easy. If all else is lost, cheat. Two books help enormously. *The Wordsworth Crossword Dictionary* alphabetically lists words according to their length from three letters to 19 letters while *Chambers Crossword Compiler* lists words with alternate blank letters. So, that, if, in a six-letter answer, you have the letters 'a-b-c-', it will suggest 'abbacy'. It is also helpful if your word starts with a blank. You can look up '-a-b-c' and it will give you 'iambic'. Online, www.oneacross.com, allows you to pick a word of any length. Fill in the letters you have already got and it will come up with a range of suggestions. Ultimately, at www.crosswordsolver.org, cruciverbalists pick each other's brains. Among the national daily newspapers, *The Times* has the best crossword. Here are three outstanding clues:

What makes Californians Californians, backing the country? [7]. *Answer* 'Senegal', a country, which, when backed [reversed] gives 'LA genes'. Los Angeles genes give the people of LA their distinctive qualities.

Doctor's enemy drank, but never managed to hold drink [5]. *Answer* 'Dalek', The Doctor's enemy. Drank, but never managed: 'managed' = 'ran'. So, 'drank' without 'ran' = 'dk'. If drink is ale, 'dk' holding 'ale' is Dalek.

What may up deliveries of vegetable supreme en cocotte [8, 7]. *Answer,* 'Speaking Trumpet'. The vegetable is 'pea'; supreme is 'king'; a cocotte was a strumpet. So, 'pea' and 'king' in 'strumpet' is 'speaking trumpet', something that may up deliveries, increase volume.

All compilers have their favourite clues. The great Tim Moorey, a member of the small team behind the Mephisto crossword in the *Sunday Times,* one of the best puzzles in Britain, likes one set in the 1960s by a compiler who was surprised to find that *Chambers Dictionary* had not by then added 'miniskirt'. His clue for 'miniskirts' was therefore: 'They should not be looked up in *Chambers Dictionary*'.

IF IT'S IDIOMATIC,
IT'S OFTEN IDIOSYNCRATIC
AND SOMETIMES IDIOTIC

English must be one of the hardest languages to learn because of our love of idiom: such phrases as 'fit as a fiddle', 'as right as rain', 'swinging the lead' to describe a malingerer and 'a tidy stretch', meaning 'quite a long distance'. What is tidy about that? I append a few other odd examples:

Apple-pie order
If everything is in 'apple-pie order', it means everything is tidy. Possibly derived from the French *'nappes pliées',* meaning 'neatly folded linen'. An old practical joke involved a bed being made with a sheet folded back on itself halfway down so the would-be occupant could not get into it properly. This was called an 'apple-pie bed'.

Kick the bucket
To die. The idea was that, if you intended to commit suicide by hanging yourself, you could stand on a bucket with a noose just above your head. Once you had placed your head in the noose and kicked the bucket away, you would throttle yourself. Cheery, eh?

The cat's pyjamas [or whiskers]
The very best. An English tailor of the late 1700s and the early 1800s made the finest silk pyjamas. The perfect apparel for a catnap? That is one suggestion anyway. In the early days of radio, a cat's-whisker receiver had a long thin wire that had to be tweaked in order to find the station you were seeking. The wire looked like a cat's whisker. This was presumably equated with 'the very best' because without the wire the radio would be useless. Cf. the bees' knees and the dog's bollocks.

Doubting Thomas
We are on firmer territory here. A doubting Thomas is a sceptic after the apostle, Thomas, who said he would not believe that Christ had risen from the dead until he had touched his wounds.

One over the eight
Slightly drunk, which is what you would be if you had had more than eight glasses of beer. But are we talking about pints or halves? If pints, then the word would better be arseholed, bladdered, canned…

Flutter the dovecotes
Startle a peaceful community. Possibly after Shakespeare's *Coriolanus:* 'like an eagle in a dove-cote, I fluttered your Volscians in Corioli'. Please read *Coriolanus* to understand what this was all about.

Run the gauntlet
To suffer a punishing ordeal. The phrase has nothing to do with a glove, but is a version of an earlier word, gantlope, which was taken from the Swedish *gatloppe* or *gantlop,* meaning a course along which to run. There was a custom in the army of making an offender run through two lines of soldiers who beat him with cudgels and sticks to show him what they thought of him.

Happy as a sandboy
Very contented. In the eighteenth and nineteenth centuries, sandboys delivered sand to pubs and theatres, where it was used as a floor covering before sawdust took its place. They were not really boys, but men of a low status. Delivering sand sounds like thirsty work and so it was. The sandboys were happy because they were usually drunk.

Ivory tower

A haven from life's stark realities or pejoratively the hiding place of a self-centred recluse. In modern times, the first usage [*tour d'ivoire*] is to be found in a poem of 1837 by one of the major figures of French literary history, Charles Saint-Beuve, to describe the intellectual isolation of the literary critic, Alfred de Vigny. Ivory was chosen, presumably, because it is an expensive, but impractical building material.

Jerry built

Badly built. The *Classical Dictionary of the Vulgar Tongue* [1811] has the word 'jerrycummumble' or 'jerrymumble', meaning 'to shake about'. That is one possible derivation. Another refers to the walls of Jericho, which came tumbling down. Or you may prefer the suggestion that it is associated with the Romany word for excrement, 'gerry'.

Kibosh [pronounced Kye-Bosh]

A restraining element. The word is of doubtful derivation. One suggestion is that it comes from the Irish, *an chaip bhais*, meaning 'the cap of death', a reference to the black cap worn by a judge when sentencing an offender to capital punishment. On the other hand, it may be connected with the Scottish 'kye booties', meaning 'cow boots', the straps put on cattle to prevent them from straying. The word lives on through performances of the 1914 music-hall song, 'When Belgium Put the Kibosh on the Kaiser', written by Alf Ellerton and sung by Mark Sheridan. At the start of the First World War, Germany invaded neutral Belgium and Luxembourg as part of a plan to capture France quickly. Technically, it was this action that took Britain into the war, as it was bound by an agreement to protect Belgium in the event of hostilities. The Belgians are still remembered for their resistance during the early days of the war with their army, which was about a tenth of the size of the German army, delaying the German offensive for nearly a month. Sheridan sang:

Belgium put the kibosh on the Kaiser.
Europe took the stick and made him sore.
On his throne it hurts to sit.
And when John Bull starts to hit,
He will never sit upon it any more.

Leave someone in the lurch
To desert someone in need of help. From the mid–1600s, 'lurch' meant 'a state of discomfiture'. It is now used only in this idiom. To be in the lurch in cribbage is to be in a losing position. At one time, lurch was itself a game, probably akin to backgammon.

As keen as mustard
Enthusiastic. Mustard was once an essential accompaniment to beef. It became associated with vigour and enthusiasm because it added zest and flavour.

Not on your Nelly
Certainly not. This is rhyming slang for 'puff' [or 'breath'] for Nelly Duff. So, not on your life. 'Tough Nellie Duff, the strong-arm schoolmarm' was a character in a children's comic in the 1930s.

Know your onions
To be extremely capable. Another idiom of doubtful provenance. One suggestion is that rhyming slang is again involved. Onions = onion rings = things. But a more likely explanation is that it emanates from America. In the 1920s, there was a collection of phrases denoting knowledgeability in a certain subject: know your apples, know your eggs, know your oats – all foods and all starting with a vowel. It is the sort of wordplay Americans enjoyed in the era of the flapper.

Beyond the pale
Socially unacceptable. 'Pale' is derived from the Latin '*palus*', meaning a stake. In the fourteenth century, stakes were used to determine boundaries between land settled by British colonists in Ireland and the rest of the country. The colonists believed that people living beyond the pale were uncivilised.

Call it quits
To abandon something and particularly to agree that a debt has been settled. Nobody is certain about the derivation, but 'quits' could come from the Latin '*quittus*', meaning 'discharged'. The word was once written on receipts to show something had been paid for.

Rain cats and dogs
To rain heavily. Here again, you can choose the derivation you like best. The idiom may be linked with the supernatural, cats associated with witches who could cause storms, dogs attendant on Odin, a god in Norse mythology, whose name was related to '*oor*', meaning 'fury'. More prosaically, when it rained hard in mediaeval times, small animals were drowned, leading some to think that their bodies had fallen from the skies. When the car maker, Datsun, was mainly based in Japan, cogs used in engines were flown to Britain where the cars were assembled. When a cargo of cogs fell from an aircraft hold and hurtled towards earth, some people commented: 'It's raining Datsun cogs.' [Joke.]

Sick as a parrot
Extremely disappointed, as a football manager is when his team loses. When his team wins, he is 'over the moon'. God knows where this came from, parrots being no more prone to nausea, as far as I know, than any other creature.

Steal someone's thunder
To win praise from something that should have gone to someone

else. You will like this, I think. When the dramatist, John Dennis [1658–1734] invented a way of simulating the sound of thunder in a theatre, he used it in one of his plays, which had only a brief run. Shortly afterwards, he saw a performance of *Macbeth,* in which his invention was recreated without credit. His reaction: 'Damn them. They will not let my play run, but they steal my thunder.'

Bob's your uncle
Problem solved. The usual explanation is that, when the young Arthur Balfour [1848–1930] was appointed Chief Secretary of Ireland by his uncle, the Prime Minister, Lord [Robert] Salisbury [1830–1903], opposition MPs proclaimed: Bob's your uncle, meaning that his uncle would give him anything he wanted. The difficulty with this explanation is that the phrase first became current in the 1930s.

Vent one's spleen
Show one's anger. For centuries, it was thought that your spleen, the organ that filters blood, harboured rage. So that, when you lost your temper, you gave vent to your spleen.

White elephant
A useless possession which costs a lot to maintain. The kings of Siam, now Thailand, once kept rare albino elephants, which were regarded as holy and whose upkeep was expensive. The kings sometimes gave a white elephant to a courtier they disliked in the hope that the recipient would lose all his money trying to maintain the animal.

Young Turks
People in an organisation seeking prominence and power. The original Young Turks belonged to an early twentieth-century political party in Turkey that favoured the reformation of the monarchy of the Ottoman empire.

Aa   HOW TO WIN AT SCRABBLE

Some people who do not play Scrabble think that you need to know many long words in order to win. Long words are not, in fact, as useful as short ones. The use of two-letter words can help you make a number of words in one go. Apart from the well-known ones *[ah, am, an, as, at, ay, be, by, do, eh, er, go, ha, he, hi, if, in, is, it, lo, ma, me, no, of, oh, on, or, ow, ox, pa, pi, so, ta, to, um, up, we* and *ye]*, there are 64 lesser-known ones:

A

Aa..A type of volcanic rock
Ab ....A month in the Jewish calendar
Ad ....An advertisement
Ae................................A Scottish word meaning 'one'
Ag................................ The chemical symbol for silver
Ai..A sloth with three toes
Al......................... The chemical symbol for aluminium
Ar ....The eighteenth letter of the English alphabet
Aw....An American word, expressing disappointment or sympathy
Ax.. Same as 'axe'

B

Ba....................... The soul in ancient Egyptian religion
Bi..Bisexual
Bo....................................An American word for 'man'

D

De.. 'From' or 'away'

E

Ea ....A river
Ed...Editor
Ef................................... The sixth letter of the English alphabet
El .... An elevated railroad
Em ....A printer's measure as wide as the letter 'm'
En ....A printer's measure as wide as the letter 'n'
.... In other words, half the width of an em
Es...........................The nineteenth letter of the English alphabet
Et...Dialect word for 'ate'
Ex ....Former spouse

F

Fa .... The fourth note in the tonic sol-fa scale
Fe ....Same as 'fee'

H

Hm...Expression of hesitation or doubt
Ho ....A call for attention

I

Id .... A fish

J

Jo ....A Scottish word meaning 'beloved one'

K

Ka............................... Spirit or soul [Ancient Egyptian]
Ki...Life force
Ky .... Scots word for 'cows'

L

La ....The sixth note in the tonic sol-fa scale
Li .... The Chinese equivalent of about a third of a mile

M

Mi....................................The third note of the tonic sol-fa scale
Mm ....Expression of enjoyment
Mo.. Archaic word for more
Mu.. The Greek letter 'm'

N

Na .... Scottish form of 'no'
Ne..Obsolete word for 'not'
Nu .... The Greek letter 'n'

Id

Qi

O

Ob ....Obsolete word for 'objection'
Od ....A mild oath
Oe .... A Scottish grandchild
Oi ....A call for attention
Om ....Sacred Hindu chant
Op .... Surgical operation
Os ....Bone
Oy .... Another Scottish grandchild

P

Pe ....Ratio between price and earnings

Q

Qi ....Life force

R

Re ....About

S

Sh ....A call for silence
Si ....The same as 'te'[see overleaf]

T

Te ....The seventh note in the tonic sol-fa scale
Ti... [As above]

U

Un ....Dialect for 'one'
Ut .... First note of the musical scale, now generally 'doh'

W

Wo ....Variant of 'woe' or 'whoa'

X

Xi .... The Greek letter 'x'
Xu .... Vietnamese money

Y

Ya ....'You'
Yo .... A call for attention [as in George Bush's 'Yo, Blair']

Z

Za... Pizza

Wo

'K' and 'v' are particularly irksome letters for Scrabble players. So, it is helpful to memorise three–letter words that use them. Putting to one side *keg, ken, key, kid, kin, kip, kir and kit* we have: *kab, kae, kaf, kai, kak, kam, kas, kat, kaw, kay, kea, keb, ked, kef, kep, ket, kif, kis, koa, kob, koi, kon, kop, kor, kos, kue and kyu*. ....

Three-letter words with 'k' as the middle letter include *eke, ski* and *sky*. In addition, there are: *aka, ake, oka, oke* and *ska*.
....
Three-letter words that have 'k' as their last letter include *ark, ask, auk, elk, ilk, ink, irk, oak, wok and yak*. Others are: *eek, lek, rok* and *tsk*. ....
....
Dealing with 'v' in the same way, three-letter words that have it as their first letter include *van, vat, vet, vex, via, vie, vim, vow* and *vox*. There are also: *vac, vae, vag, var, vas, vav, vaw, vee, veg, vid, vig, vis, vly, voe, vol, vug* and *vum*.

Three-letter words with 'v' as the middle letter include *ave, eve, ivy* and *ova*. Add to them only: *ava*, a Polynesian shrub.

Three-letter words that have 'v' as their last letter include *lav, luv* and *rev*. Others are: *gov, guv* and *lev*.

In all, there are 143,000 words you are allowed to use in Scrabble – from '*aa*' to '*zymotically*'.

No list is definitive. Electronic games I have played recently [what a saddo!] accept '*ja*' and '*zo*'.

FOREIGN TONGUES,
MANY DISAPPEARING

Across the world, there are about 6,000 languages, but the figure
is falling. In the next 200 years, half of our languages will be lost.
Within Britain, at least three could go: Scottish Gaelic, currently
spoken by about 60,000 people; Guernsey French, which has
about 1,300 speakers; and Cornish, understood by about 500
people, but no longer spoken by anyone. Among endangered
languages, Welsh is considered merely vulnerable because of
support from the Welsh Assembly.

At least three languages have disappeared in the past generation.
Manx was obliterated when its last known speaker, Ned Maddrell,
a fisherman, died in 1974; more recently, the Alaskan language,
Eyak, vanished with the death of its last speaker in 2009; and the
Bo language disappeared when the last Bo-speaking member of
the Bo tribe in the Indian-owned Andaman Islands died in 2010.
About 130 languages are each spoken by fewer than ten people.
One is the Indonesian language of Dusner. This language began
to die out when people realised that their children stood a better
chance of getting a job or going to university if they spoke Malay,
Indonesia's main language. One feature of Dusner is that its
number system is in base five. So, 'six', '*rindi yoser*', is a
combination of the words for 'five', '*rindi*', and 'one', '*yoser*'.
Until October 2010, there were four speakers. Then, Mount
Merapi, a volcano on the border between central Java and
the city of Yogyakarta [or Yogjakarta or Jogjakarta] erupted.
The Indonesian government advised everyone living in the area
to leave. But one woman who spoke Dusner was unable to go.
She was one of 350 victims of the eruptions. At about the same
time, another speaker died in flash floods in the village of Dusner.
Linguisticians from Oxford University then spent three months
speaking to and recording on video the last two speakers,
persuading them to tell stories and jokes.

The European Union has a project called the European Language Diversity for All programme, which is designed to protect the most threatened native tongues. It has received 2.7 million Euros to identify languages most at risk. But some experts are unconcerned. One said that cultural change is driving the process. The argument runs: if people do not use a language any more, it is no longer a language.

Some futurologists say that in time the world will have only three languages, English, Spanish and Mandarin.

ENGLISH FROM GERMAN

Abseil
An adaptation of *'abseilen'*, to rope down, a facet of mountaineering. The most famous abseiling incident in Britain involved a group of lesbian demonstrators invading a BBC television studio transmitting the *Six O'Clock News* the night before the enactment of a law prohibiting local authorities from 'promoting' homosexuality. Nicholas Witchell physically tackled the women, but even that did not endear him to the Prince of Wales.

Blitz
An abbreviation of 'Blitzkrieg', lightning war, first used here to describe the devastating air-raids made on London in 1940.

Creutzfeldt-Jakob disease
Named after two German neurologists, Hans Creutzfeldt and Alfons Jakob, this is a human form of mad cow disease.

Diktat
The noun equivalent of 'dictate': a strict command.

Ersatz
Originally, compensation or replacement. Now, an inferior version of the real thing.

Flak
An acronym: *FlugAbwehrKanone*, anti-aircraft fire from ground-based artillery. Now widened to denote criticism.

Creutzfeldt-Jakob disease

Glockenspiel

Literally, bell play. A musical instrument in which small bells are struck by levers operated from a keyboard.

Hinterland

Behind land or a district lying a short distance from the coast or a major port. Interestingly broadened now to signify an interest set apart from one's main concern. The elder statesman, Lord Healey, once said all politicians should have a hinterland in readiness for the day on which they no longer had power. Healey had photography and the poetry of Emily Dickinson.

Infobahn

After *Autobahn,* a motorway. Infobahn is the information superhighway. In other words, that function of the Internet that supplies information. [So, the Germans have portmanteau words too. See page 97.]

Jawohl

Yes, indeed, but used comically as if to say 'Your orders will be obeyed'.

Kraut

Literally, cabbage. Mostly an abusive term for the Germans in the Second World War.

Leitmotiv

In musical and literary parlance, a theme.

Meistersinger

A musician known for his elaborate technique.

Nazi
An abbreviation of Nationalsozialist, a member of the National Socialist Workers' Party.

Ostpolitik
'*Ost*' means East and '*Politik*' means policy. So, German policy on Eastern Europe.

Poltergeist
Noisy ghost.

Qualitätswein
Wine of quality, one up from *vin ordinaire*.

Rottweiler
An unpleasant dog, apparently named after Rottweil, a town in south-west Germany.

Schadenfreude
Harm and joy. The enjoyment of other people's misfortunes, such as the laughter triggered by someone slipping on a banana skin. There is no direct English translation.

Nor is there for '*gemütlich*'. The nearest is 'cosy' or 'congenial', but neither sums up the essence of '*gemutlich*'. Also without direct translations are '*vorgestern*' and '*ubermorgen*', the day before yesterday and the day after tomorrow.

[O] Tannenbaum
Originally, a folk song; then, a carol, and the Socialists' anthem, 'The Red Flag': 'the workers' flag is deepest red' etc. A '*Tannenbaum*' is a Christmas tree.

Vorsprung durch Technik
Progress through engineering, a highly successful slogan employed
by Audi cars.

Wanderlust
A desire for travelling.

Zeitgeist
Literally, time spirit. The spirit that marks the feeling of an age.

If the law of accession to the throne, which discriminated against
women, had been abolished in the nineteenth century, Kaiser
Wilhelm of Germany may well have become King of England.
Queen Victoria's eldest child was the Princess Royal, also
christened Victoria. In 1858, she married Prince Friedrich
Wilhelm of Prussia, later Frederich III, German Emperor and
King of Prussia. They had four sons and four daughters, the eldest
of whom was Wilhelm. Had the Princess Royal been allowed to
succeed Queen Victoria in 1901, her reign would have been short
as she survived her mother by only a few months. The crown
would then have passed to Wilhelm. So, if Britain and Germany
had been linked in that way, there might have been no First World
War, no rise of Nazism in Germany, no Hitler and no Second
World War.

ARE YOU ABOUT TO SUFFER DEMENTIA?

In the 1970s, ten questions were asked of elderly patients to determine whether they were beginning to suffer from dementia:

- How old are you?
- What is the time [to the nearest hour]?
- What is your address?
- Which year are we in?
- What is the name of this hospital?
- Do you recognise two people present?
- What is your date of birth?
- When did World War One begin?
- Who is the present monarch?
- Count backwards from twenty to one.

> ***True story:*** *the wife of one patient asked how many questions you had to get right to be deemed free of risk. She was told 'seven'. She admitted she got only three right.*

The test was replaced by one in which a patient was given a piece of paper with a circle of 10cm diameter drawn on it. The patient was told to imagine that the circle was a clock face and then add the numbers and the hands indicating that the time was 10.50. Marks were awarded relating to which and how many numbers had been put down, whether an attempt had been made to give the time and whether one hand was shown to be longer than the other.

WORDS SHAKESPEARE INVENTED

Assassination
Macbeth
'If the assassination could trammel up the consequence.'

Baseless
The Tempest
'The baseless fabric of this vision.'

Castigate
Timon of Athens
'If thou didst put this sour cold habit on to castigate thy pride, 'twere well.'

Dwindle
Henry IV part I
'Am I not fallen away since this last action? Do I not bate? Do I not dwindle?'

Exposure
Troilus and Cressida
'To weaken and discredit our exposure.'

Frugal
The Merry Wives of Windsor
'I was then frugal of my mirth.'

Gloomy
Titus Andronicus
'The ruthless, vast and gloomy woods.'

Impartial
Richard II
'Impartial are our eyes and ears.'

Lonely
Coriolanus
'I go alone like to a lonely dragon.'

Monumental
Othello
'Skin smooth as monumental alabaster.'

Negotiate
Much Ado About Nothing
'Let every eye negotiate for itself and trust no agent.'

Obscene
Richard II
'So heinous, black, obscene a deed.'

Premeditated
A Midsummer Night's Dream
'Greet me with premeditated welcomes.'

Radiance
All's Well That Ends Well
'In his bright radiance and collateral light must I be comforted.'

Submerge
Antony and Cleopatra
'So half my Egypt were submerged.'

Tranquil
Othello
'Farewell, the tranquil mind, farewell, content.'

Unreal
Macbeth
'Hence horrible shadow, unreal mockery hence.'

Varied
Titus Andronicus
'Where like a sweet melodious bird it sung sweet varied notes enchanting every ear.'

Worthless
Titus Andronicus
'Methinks I do digress too much, crying my worthless praise.'

Shakespeare died on the same day as Cervantes. Can you not hear a modern British newsreader? '*Two major literary figures have died – William Shakespeare, the greatest English playwright, and Miguel de Cervantes, who wrote* Don Quixote, *the first modern novel.*'

PHRASES SHAKESPEARE INVENTED

All that glitters isn't gold
Merchant of Venice
The original was 'all that glisters is not gold'.

Be-all and end-all
Macbeth
'This blow might be the be-all and end-all'.

[The] Course of true love never did run smooth
A Midsummer Night's Dream
'For aught I could ever read, could ever hear by tale of history,
the course of true love never did run smooth.'

[Every] Dog will have its day
Hamlet
'Let Hercules himself do what he may. The cat will mew and dog
will have his day.'

Eat out of house and home
Henry IV Part II
'He hath eaten me out of house and home. He hath put all my
substance into that fat belly of his.'

Foregone conclusion
Othello
'But this denoted a foregone conclusion: 'tis a shrewd doubt,
though it may be a dream.'

Green-eyed monster
Othello
'O beware, my lord, of jealousy. It is the green-eyed monster, which doth mock the meat it feeds on.'

Heart of gold
Henry V
'The king's a bawcock (a fine fellow) and a heart of gold, a lad of life, an imp of fame.'

It's [all] Greek to me
Julius Caesar
The original was 'it was Greek to me'.

Knock, knock. Who's there?
Macbeth
'Knock, knock, knock! Who's there i' th' name of Beelzebub?'

Live-long day
Julius Caesar
'Your infant in your arms and there have sat the live-long day with patient expectation.'

Method in his madness
Hamlet
'Though this be madness, yet there is method in it.'

Neither a borrower nor a lender be
Hamlet
'Neither a borrower nor a lender be for loan oft loses both itself and friend.'

One fell swoop
Macbeth
'What, all my pretty chickens and their dam? Oh, hell kite! All? At one fell swoop.' Macduff was asking if all his pretty chickens (his children) and their dam (mother) were killed by Macbeth (the predatory kite) at one fell swoop (in one fatal stroke; at one go). Often misquoted as 'one foul swoop'.

Strange bedfellows
The Tempest
'Misery acquaints a man with strange bedfellows.'

Too much of a good thing
As You Like It
'Can one desire too much of a good thing.'

Wear one's heart on one's sleeve
Othello
'But I will wear my heart upon my sleeve for daws (birds) to peck at.'

THE COMFORT OF CATCH PHRASES

The old-time radio comic, Ted Ray, had a high-powered reminder of the importance of catch phrases. In his weekly show, *Ray's a Laugh* [1949–61], there was always a reference to someone's 'big red conk [nose]'. After a while, it was dropped. When Ted was introduced to George VI at a *Royal Command Film Performance*, the king asked him:

> *'Why have you changed your show?'*
> *'In what way, Your Majesty?'*
> *'You have dropped some of your catch phrases.*
> *What has happened to "look at your big red conk"?'*
> *'We took it out because some housewives objected*
> *to it. They said some of their children were using it*
> *disrespectfully to their parents.'*
> *'Pity! I did so much look forward to that every week.'*

In comedy shows through the years, catch phrases have never been funny in themselves (and most of the current generation seem to have rebelled against them as too easy a way of getting a laugh) but they do appear to be comforting.

Always merry and bright

A line from 'My Motter' [Motto] by the far from merry Alfred Lester in the musical comedy, *The Arcadians*. Quoted by Somerset Maugham and P. G. Wodehouse, it found its way into the language.

Beautiful downtown Burbank

A tongue-in-cheek reference to the district of Los Angeles, from where NBC transmitted the quickfire *Rowan and Martin's Laugh-In* [1968–73].

Do you come here often?

A genuine chat-up line in the 1940s, it was voiced by Spike Milligan in *The Goon Show* [1951–60], the answer being 'Only in the mating season'.

Cry all the way to the bank

When the outrageous American pianist-cum-perjurer, Liberace, was asked in the 1950s if he was ashamed to earn large amounts of money for just playing the piano, he replied, 'Oh, yes, I cry all the way to the bank.' It became his catch phrase.

Exit stage left

A frequent saying of the would-be actor, Snagglepuss, an American cartoon character who appeared in a number of shows from 1959 onwards.

Flobbadob [or, come to that, Flibbadob]

Part of the personal language of the puppets, Bill and Ben, in the children's television series, *The Flowerpot Men* [1952–4]. The voices of Bill, Ben and others were supplied by Peter Hawkins [1924–2006].

Goodnight, children, everywhere

The closing words of Uncle Mac [Derek McCulloch] on BBC Radio's *Children's Hour* [1922–64]. Before making his name as an electronic music composer, my late brother, John, was the studio manager on one of Uncle Mac's broadcasts. After reciting those famous valedictory words, Uncle Mac's microphone was faded out. He turned to John and said, 'That should keep the little bastards quiet for another week.'

He's from Barcelona

An apology offered by Basil Fawlty, played by John Cleese, in BBC Television's *Fawlty Towers*, for the poor English spoken by a Spanish waiter, Manuel, played by Andrew Sachs. After the programme had been sold to Spain, the line was dubbed to mean 'He's from Rome.'

I know nothing

The claim by Sergeant Hans Schultz in the television series, *Hogan's Heroes*, set in a German prison camp in the Second World War.

Just like that

Frequently used by the comedy magician, Tommy Cooper, often wearing a fez, when he performed a trick correctly [or, as often as not incorrectly]. Once, when Cooper took a foreign holiday, he visited a market and tried on a fez at one of the stalls. Straightaway, the stallholder said 'Just like that.' Cooper wanted to know how he was aware of his catch phrase. The man knew neither Cooper nor his catch phrase. Suffice it to say that, whenever an English holidaymaker stopped at his stall and tried on a fez, someone said 'Just like that.'

Know what I mean, Harry?

When Frank Bruno was a well-known boxer in the late 1980s, he often gave interviews to the BBC boxing commentator, Harry Carpenter, during which this question became a catch phrase. Bruno nurtured a self-deprecatory wit usually unknown in sportsmen. It accounted for his later success as a pantomime performer.

Lloyd George knew my father

At first, a proud piece of namedropping and then a lyric sung to the tune of 'Onward, Christian Soldiers' ['Lloyd George knew my father, Father knew Lloyd George' ad infinitum.]

My husband and I

This saying was used so frequently by the Queen when describing her foreign travels with the Duke of Edinburgh that it started to become something of a joke. So Her Majesty changed the form of words to 'Prince Philip and I'. However, on her twenty-fifth wedding anniversary in 1972, she said, 'I think everyone will concede that on this of all days I should begin my speech with "My husband and I".'

Only gay in the village

The proud boast of the committed 'homosexualist', Daffyd, played by Matt Lucas in BBC Television's *Little Britain*. Daffyd auditioned for a production of *Hamlet* by the Llanddewi Brefi Amateur Dramatics Society by performing the Weather Girls' hit, 'It's Raining Men'. When he was turned down, he accused the company of being 'homophobist'.

Never give a sucker an even break

The catch phrase of W. C. Fields, who used it in the movie, *Poppy* [1936], although possibly not for the first time. It amounts to: 'Forget all scruples. Just keep ahead of everyone.'

Peel me a grape

In *I'm No Angel* [1933], an angry admirer walks out on Mae West. She shrugs, turns to her maid and says, 'Beulah, peel me a grape.'

Resistance is futile

The catch phrase of the alien, The Borg, in *Star Trek: the Next Generation* [1987–94].

Smile. You're on Candid Camera

The instruction to a victim of a practical joke perpetrated on the television show, *Candid Camera*, which ran from 1948 into the 1980s.

Wakey, wakey!

The cry of the band-leader, Billy Cotton [1900–69] at the start of his radio and television shows.

You ain't heard nothing yet

From 1906 onwards, the catch phrase of the self-promoting American singer, Al Jolson [1886–1950], who liked nothing better than entertaining audiences. To the dismay of one of his brides, he even did a show on his wedding day.

That's all, folks

The sign-off by Porky Pig at the end of the *Looney Tunes* cartoons produced by Warner Brothers. Porky's voice was supplied by Mel Blanc [1908–99], who made a career out of lending voices to cartoon characters. 'That's all, folks' is even inscribed on his tombstone.

RULES: SOME TO OBEY

Absolute Adjectives
An example of this is 'unique', a word that cannot be qualified.
Nothing can be 'rather unique' or 'more unique'. It is either
unique or it is not. Other absolutes are 'eternal', 'supreme'
and 'unanimous'.

The apostrophe will probably disappear within the next 50 years
or so. That will provide great relief to a future generation of
greengrocers whose modern-day counterparts now find it so
troublesome, using it to mangle perfectly straightforward plurals,
'tomato's', 'bean's' and 'pea's', for example. The rules are not that
difficult. Firstly, an apostrophe should be used to show that a word
has been shortened: 'the book's been stolen' instead of 'the book
has been stolen'. Secondly, it indicates possession: 'the book's
pages; the book's chapters' – the pages of the book, the chapters
of the book. If more than one book is involved, refer to 'the
books' pages', placing the apostrophe after the 's'. Some people
are tripped up when the plural noun does not end in 's', such as
'women'. Then, it is 'the women's books'. Finally, never use an
apostrophe in possessive pronouns, such as 'hers', 'its' and 'yours'.

Between you and me
Some people feel uncomfortable about using this phrase because
they think it sounds more educated to say 'between you and I'.
But the 'me' version is right. 'Between' is a preposition. 'I' and 'me'
are pronouns, 'I' a subjective pronoun and 'me' an objective one.
Pronouns that follow prepositions are always objective.

'Compare to' or 'compare with'?
You compare one thing to another to illustrate that they are
similar. You compare one thing with another to show there
are differences. When Shakespeare wrote 'Shall I compare thee
to a summer's day?' he was indicating there was a likeness, even
though he believed 'Thou art more lovely and more temperate.'

Different from or to?
Latinists insist on 'from'. It does not matter. What is ugly is 'different than'.

'Flammable' the same as 'inflammable'?
No. A flammable substance will burn. An inflammable one will burn very quickly. The prefix 'in' is derived from a Greek word meaning 'very'. This contrasts with such words as 'inaccessible' where 'in' is derived from Latin and means 'not'.

Friendly, friendlier, friendliest
If there are two dogs, one may ask 'Which is the friendlier?' If there are more than two, the question has to be 'Which is the friendliest?'

Hung and hanged
A picture is hung. A man is hanged. To his discredit, Alan Jay Lerner gave this line in *My Fair Lady* to the English-language expert, Professor Higgins, when speaking of his protégée, Eliza Doolittle: 'She should be taken out and hung for the cold-blooded murder of the English tongue.' At the first-night party in London, Noël Coward bore down on Lerner with just one word: 'Hung?' When engaged on his frequent Middle East peace missions, Henry Kissinger attracted the attention of a graffiti artist who wrote: 'Kissinger should be bloody well hung.' Someone added: 'He is, my dear. He is.'

Imply or infer?
This is merely active compared with passive. I imply that a grammatical rule is correct. You infer from what I say that it is.

Less and fewer
Less is applied to a singular mass noun. For example, 'less rain'. With plural nouns, use fewer as in 'fewer raindrops'. Supermarkets that display signs near their tills saying 'Less than five items' are wrong. 'Fewer than five items' is the correct phrase.

May or might?

'He may have won' means that he possibly won. It is not known whether he did or not. 'He might have won' means that it was once thought that he could win, but he failed to. A television bulletin reported that 'a smoke alarm may have saved the life of a woman'. In fact, the woman died because she did not have a smoke alarm. In other words, if a smoke alarm had been installed, it might have saved her life.

'Only', a word that limits

So, it has to be placed as close as it can to the thing that it is limiting. 'He only did it because he wanted to' probably means 'He did it only because he wanted to'. The limiting refers to the wanting rather than the doing. Take this sentence: 'The driver broke his leg'. Place the word 'only' before 'the driver', 'broke' and 'his leg' and see how the meaning changes.

'Ow', pronounced 'Ough'

Who says the English language is easy to learn? Take the four letters 'ough'. They can be pronounced ow, aw, off, oh, up, ock and oo, as in bough, bought, cough, dough, hiccough, lough and through.

Round and around

Round the world or around the world? In general, we say 'round' in Britain and 'around' in America.

'Try to' or 'try and'?

'To try to do' indicates an attempt to make something work. 'Try and' signifies that the attempt is somehow separate from the action. So, always 'try to'.

Which and that

Use 'that' when the item in question is being defined. Use 'which' when additional information is being given.

RULES: THOSE TO IGNORE

AVOID CLICHÉS LIKE THE PLAGUE
.
BE MORE OR LESS SPECIFIC
.
ESCHEW AMPERSANDS & ABBREVIATIONS, ETC.
.
NEVER USE A BIG WORD WHEN A
DIMINUTIVE ONE WOULD SUFFICE
.
USE THE APOSTROPHE IN IT'S PROPER PLACE
AND OMIT IT WHEN ITS NOT NEEDED
.
NEVER GENERALISE
.
PROOFREAD CAREFULLY TO SEE
IF YOU ANY WORDS OUT

We can forget about the one that decrees:
Prepositions are what you shouldn't end sentences with:

In Henry V, *the Earl of Exeter says:*
'Scorn and defiance; slight regard, contempt
And anything that may not misbecome.
The mighty sender, doth he prize you at.'

DIVIDED BY A COMMON LANGUAGE

Most people attribute the notion that Britain and America are divided by a common language to Shaw. A book of humorous sayings, published in 1935, quotes him thus: 'England and America are two countries separated by the same language.' But no source is given. However, Wilde, in his novel, *The Canterville Ghost* [1887], opined: 'We really have everything in common with America nowadays except, of course, language.' Bertrand Russell agreed: 'It is a misfortune for Anglo–American friendship that the two countries are supposed to have a common language' [1944]. Shortly before his death in 1953, Dylan Thomas said that European writers and scholars in America were 'up against the barrier of a common language.' We can add to this mix Winston Churchill who was quoted by *The Times* [1987] and *The European* [1991] as saying that 'our countries are divided by a common language.'

Here is a smattering of what they were on about:

English	**American**
Anorak [the raiment, not the person]	Parka
Biscuit	Cookie
Catherine wheel	Pinwheel
Disorientated	Disoriented
Estate car	Station wagon
Fag [cigarette]	Gay man [pejorative]
Gymkhana	Horse show
Holiday	Vacation
Inheritance tax	Estate tax
Joe Bloggs	Joe Blow
Kennel	Dog house
Lavatory	Rest room
Mobile phone	Cell phone
Neat [of a drink]	Straight

Off-licence .... Liquor store
Pneumatic drill .... Jackhammer
Queue .... Line
Shopping centre .... Mall
Tower block .... High-rise
Underground [train] .... Subway
Walking stick .... Cane
Yeti .... Bigfoot
Zip .... Zipper

LOST IN TRANSLATION

When the late Elizabeth Taylor flew into London in the 1950s, reporters at Heathrow shouted at her: 'How are you?' 'I'm feeling like a million dollars,' she replied. The next morning, the *Daily Telegraph* translated her response: 'I'm feeling like £357,000.'

A Massachusetts newspaper installed a computer programme that automatically changed reporters' references to black people to the preferred term, African-American. Not long afterwards, this paragraph appeared: 'Governor Dukakis pledged to get the state's economy back into the African-American next year.'

> **True story:** *a production team shooting a film suddenly found they needed a large crowd of Japanese extras talking to each other. [Don't they plan these things?] A crowd of English extras was quickly assembled, but a phrase, used repeatedly, was needed to make them sound Japanese. Someone suggested 'I tie your shoe. You tie my shoe.' It worked.*

PORTMANTEAU WORDS

Lewis Carroll invented the expression, which describes the fusion of two words. In *Through the Looking Glass*, Humpty Dumpty explains to Alice the coinage of the unusual words in 'Jabberwocky'. 'Slithy' means 'lithe' and 'slimy' and 'mimsy' is 'flimsy' and 'miserable'. 'It's like a portmanteau,' he says. 'There are two meanings packed into one word.' Nowadays, the English language abounds with portmanteau words:

Avionics
The electronic equipment on an aircraft [aviation and electronics]

Breathalyser
The device that works out how much alcohol is in someone's blood [breath and analyser]

Chortle
Chuckle and snort [Carroll's invention]

Dumbfound
Pre-Carroll, 17th century, meaning astonish [dumb and confound]

Emoticon
A face inserted in an e-mail [emotion and icon]

Fortnight
Pre-Carroll, fourteen days [and fourteen nights]

Galumph
Stride exultantly [gallop and triumph. Another Carroll invention]

Hassle
Harass [haggle and tussle]

Interpol
Worldwide anti-crime organisation [International Criminal Police Commission]

Jaywalker
Someone crossing a road at a dangerous point. [Jay, in American slang, is an idiot]

Knowledgebase
A collection of specialist knowledge [knowledge and database]

WIRELESS	+	FIDELITY	=	WIFI
CHUCKLE	+	SNORT	=	CHORTLE
OXFORD	+	CAMBRIDGE	=	OXBRIDGE
PICTURE	+	ELEMENT	=	PIXEL
NAPHTHENE	+	PALMITATE	=	NAPALM

Laundromat
A shop where people pay to use washing machines [laundry and automatic]

Modem
A box that connects a personal computer to the telephone system [modulator and demodulator]

Napalm
A jelly used in bombs [naphthene and palmitate]

Oxbridge
Upper-class higher education [Oxford and Cambridge]

Pixel
The smallest element in a video display [picture and element]

Quasar
A source of radiation outside our galaxy [quasi-stellar]

Stagflation
An economic dilemma, in which unemployment and the rate of inflation is high and economic growth slows down. Coined in 1965 by the Conservative politician, Iain MacLeod, who was appointed Chancellor of the Exchequer five years later, less than a fortnight before he died [stagnation and inflation]

Telethon
A long television programme used to raise money for charity [television and marathon]

Wi-Fi
Computer system that does not require connecting wires [wireless and fidelity]

TXT

In a generation's time, text-speak will have been fully integrated into the English language. As of now, the *Oxford English Dictionary* has acknowledged only two terms: **LOL** [laugh out loud] and **OMG** [Oh, my God!]. [The *OED* defines LOL as 'an interjection used chiefly in electronic communications to draw attention to a joke or humorous statement or to express amusement'.] There are bound to follow **b4,** before; **brb,** be right back; **btw,** by the way; **cu,** see you; **fyi,** for your information; **gr8,** great; **l8r,** later; **m8,** mate; **rofl,** rolling on the floor laughing; **str8,** straight; and **thx,** thanks. And possibly: **afk,** away from keyboard; **cbb,** can't be bothered; **dw,** don't worry; **imo,** in my opinion; **stfu,** shut the fuck up; **tbh,** to be honest; and **wth,** what the hell.

Texting has its detractors. A leading journalist called texters vandals who are 'pillaging our punctuation, savaging our sentences (and) raping our punctuation.' An academic said it masked dyslexia, poor spelling and mental laziness: 'Texting is penmanship for illiterates.'

David Crystal, our most learned and entertaining of writers on English, is a defender. He points out that the most noticeable feature of texting is the use of single letters, numerals and symbols to represent words, such as **'b'** for 'be' and **'2'** for 'to'. But this is nothing new. An old word puzzle posed:

YY UR YY UB I C UR YY 4 ME

The translation was:
'Too wise you are. Too wise you be. I see you are too wise for me.'

People sending telegrams in the 1890s used abbreviated words:
How r u ts mng? *[How are you this morning?]*
I'm pty wl, hw r u? *[I'm pretty well. How are you?]*

Some abbreviated words have been in the language for ages: bus, cox, exam, fridge and vet, for example. In 1942, Eric Partridge published a dictionary of abbreviations. It included **'agn'** for 'again', **'mth'** for 'month' and **'gd'** for 'good'.

The initialising of common phrases has been going on for centuries. **IOU** goes back to 1618. **LOL*** is only a resonance of the lovers' code, **SWALK:** sealed with a loving kiss. [Cf Alan Bennett's **NORWICH:** knickers off ready when I come home. OK. Forget the 'k'.]

* I am told that the French version is *'mdr'* : *'mort de rire'*, 'died of laughing'.

QUOTABLE QUOTES

Kingsley Amis:
For better or worse, twentieth century music is like paedophilia. No matter how persuasively and persistently its champions urge their cause, it will never be accepted by the public at large, who will continue to regard it with incomprehension, outrage and repugnance.

Terence Blacker:
No one involved in creative work feels as appreciated as he should be, but who cares? It is the work that matters.

John Cleese in *A Fish Called Wanda*:
Do you have any idea what it's like being English? Being so correct all the time? Being so stifled by this dread of doing the wrong thing?

Claud Cockburn:
An editor has no business worrying himself sick about what the
public want. He should be thinking about perfecting and producing
what he wants and then making the public want it too.

Shirley Conran:
Life is too short to stuff a mushroom.

Noël Coward on being asked for his views about a show
starring an overacting, overexuberant young girl. At one point
in the show, a horse covered the stage in manure:
If they'd stuffed the child's head up the horse's arse, they would have
solved two problems at once.

Nancy Cunard on being greeted by a ship's steward she had
slept with the previous night:
In the circles in which I move, sexual intercourse does not constitute
an introduction.

The Duke of Edinburgh alongside the Queen who was
asking a teenage army cadet blinded in an IRA bombing
about how much sight he had left:
Not a lot, judging by the tie he's wearing.

Sir James Goldsmith:
The trouble with marrying your mistress is that it creates a vacancy.

Gilbert Harding:
This may well be apochryphal, but the story goes on being
asked to sound 'a bit more sexy' when interviewing Mae West:
If, sir, I possessed, as you suggest, the power of conveying unlimited
sexual attraction through my voice, I would not be reduced to accepting
a miserable pittance from the BBC for interviewing a faded female in
a damp basement.

Robert Helpmann, when young and effete, on being told by a muscle-bound surfer on Bondi beach that he hated homosexuality: *Well, if it doesn't work for you, dear, why not try heterosexuality?*

Steve Jobs, Apple visionary:
I skate to where the puck is going to be, not to where it has been.

Charles Kennedy suggesting a voicemail recording for Paddy Ashdown:
Please leave a message after the high moral tone.

Dr. Henry Kissinger:
Power is the ultimate aphrodisiac.

Alan J. Lerner on being asked by Andrew Lloyd Webber why people took an instant dislike to him:
It saves time.

Humphrey Lyttelton:
As we journey through life, discarding baggage along the way, we should keep an iron grip to the very end on the capacity for silliness. It preserves the soul from dessication.

Kelvin MacKenzie:
What I know about stocks and shares could safely fit up a gnat's arse.

Richard Needham, *Toronto Globe and Mail:*
As you grow old, you lose your interest in sex, your friends drift away, your children often ignore you. There are many other advantages, of course, but these would seem to be the outstanding ones.

Reinhold Niebuhr:
God, grant me the serenity to accept the things I cannot change, the courage to change things when I can and the wisdom to know the difference.

Dolly Parton on Lindsay Lohan and Britney Spears:
If those little girls slept with as many men as they say in the tabloids, their butts would have more fingerprints than the FBI.

Lord Prescott on the possibility of weapons of mass destruction in Iraq:
With hindsight, we do see that perhaps the thing is that they hadn't gone as far as they had done that, that the early stage of dealing with weapons of mass destruction had been effectively dealt with, but at that stage they are saying it's still an active part. On another occasion, Lord Prescott made much more sense: *The Green Belt is a Labour policy and we intend to build on it.*

Dave Stewart:
When people are amazing at what they do, there's usually less ego not more. I've found that to be the case with Nelson Mandela and Stevie Wonder. The big egos come with people who are pretty average. They're covering their insecurity.

Joseph Stiglitz, the Nobel Prize-winning economist, writing about the recession:
If you introduce austerity measures, the amount you can raise in tax falls and welfare payments go up. So, you don't have enough money to pay your debts anyway.

Sting:
I think I mentioned to Bob Geldof that I could make love for eight hours. What I didn't say was that this included four hours of begging and then dinner and a movie.

Lytton Strachey: During the First World War, he was accosted by a woman, who screamed at him:
Young man, why are you here when so many young men are in France fighting for civilisation? He replied: *Madam, I am the civilisation for which they are fighting.*

Tall buxom woman to whom 5'11" Charlie Drake said he would like to make love:
If you do and I find out about it, I shall be extremely annoyed.

Dylan Thomas:
An alcoholic is someone you don't like who drinks as much as you do.

Ruby Wax:
Haggis? You take the contents of a zoo, put it in a blender and then stuff it in a condom.

Lord Whitelaw, when asked at a by-election news conference about a Home Office report, said it should be considered very carefully indeed. A reporter then told him that the Conservative candidate had said it should be screwed up and thrown into a waste paper basket. Whitelaw rephrased his answer:
Quite right. It should be screwed up, thrown into a waste paper basket, then taken out, smoothed down and considered very carefully indeed.
[Possibly apochryphal.]

Lord Wilson, comparing the Labour Party to a car:
If you drive at great speed, all the people in it are either exhilarated or so sick that you have no problems. But, when you stop, they all get out and argue about which way to go.

A GAME OF TWO HALVES

Bobby Downes

Paul Gascoigne

Ron Greenwood

Stuart Pearce

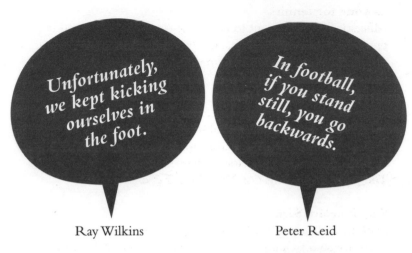

Unfortunately, we kept kicking ourselves in the foot.

Ray Wilkins

In football, if you stand still, you go backwards.

Peter Reid

But the most appealing has to be George Best's comment when he was asked where all his money had gone:

I spent quite a lot of it on booze, women and fast cars. The rest I just frittered away.

DID ANYONE EVER SAY IT?

Anyone for tennis?
[Almost]: A phrase meant to typify the paucity of invention in pre-1950s class-ridden drama. In Shaw's play, *Misalliance* [1914], someone asks 'Anyone for a game of tennis?'

Crisis? What crisis?
[No]: At the start of the Winter of Discontent [1978–79], when ambulance drivers, dustmen and sewerage workers were on strike, the Prime Minister, James Callaghan, returned to Britain from a summit meeting in Guadeloupe, denying that we were in chaos. The *Sun's* take on this was 'Crisis? What crisis?'

Play it again, Sam
[No]: In *Casablanca* [1942], Humphrey Bogart asks Dooley Wilson, cast as a club pianist, to play Herman Hupfeld's beautiful 'As Time Goes By'. His actual words were 'Play it once, Sam, for old times' sake. Play "As Time Goes By", Sam.' The misquotation became the title of a Woody Allen play in 1969 and then the movie of the play three years later.

Silly-billy
[Eventually]: A Mike Yarwood invention for the former Chancellor, Denis Healey, and pronounced a little slowly, exaggerating the first syllables of each word. Healey, never afraid to parade his sense of humour, began using the phrase frequently.

You never had it so good
[Almost]: In July 1957, the urbane Conservative Prime Minister, Harold Macmillan, addressing Conservatives in Bedford, referred to the growing prosperity of some British people. 'Let us be frank about it. Most of our people have never had it so good.'

WORDS WHOSE MEANINGS MAY BE ON THE TIP OF YOUR TONGUE

Arcane ....Understood by few
Bathos........................ A lapse from the sublime to the ridiculous
Cambric .... A fine white linen
Captious ....Carping
Casuistry.. Plausible, but flawed logic
Cupidity.. Greed
Egregious ....Outrageous
Hawser...................................A cable tying a ship to a quayside
Helot.. A serf
Hubris... Arrogance
Iconoclasm...................................... Destroying revered images
Inchoate... Unestablished
Jejune .... Immature, lacking in experience
Mountebank...Charlatan
Nemesis .... A rival who cannot be beaten
Obloquy ....Censure
Occiput.......................................The back of the head
Odalisque .... Female slave in a harem
Oxymoron ....Phrase in which contradictory words are used
Panegyric...Eulogy
Paradigm.. Basic theory
Picaresque ....Describing a likeable rogue
Shibboleth .... Slogan
Sophistry .... False reasoning
Supine.. Passive
Taxonomy ....Classification of plants or animals

WHO SPEAKS ENGLISH WHERE

Country	Speakers
United States	215,000,000
Britain	58,000,000
Canada	17,500,000
Australia	15,000,000
Irish Republic	4,000,000
Nigeria	4,000,000
New Zealand	3,500,000
Philippines	3,500,000
South Africa	3,500,000
Jamaica	2,500,000
Trinidad and Tobago	1,000,000

... and where it is spoken as an additional language

India	100,000,000
Nigeria	75,000,000
Germany	45,000,000
Philippines	45,000,000
United States	36,000,000
France	23,000,000
Pakistan	18,000,000
Italy	17,000,000
Japan	15,000,000
The Netherlands	14,000,000
Spain	12,500,000
Turkey	12,000,000
Poland	11,000,000
China	10,000,000
South Africa	10,000,000

The world's population is 7,000 million. 1,400 million people [20%] can speak English with some level of competence.

WORLDLY WORDS OF WISDOM

THE **AUTUMN** CHILL IS THE FIRST THING
FELT BY A THIN PERSON
China

·

NEVER **BOLT** YOUR DOOR WITH
A BOILED CARROT
Ireland

·

THE ONE ON WHOSE HEAD WE WOULD
BREAK A **COCONUT** NEVER STANDS STILL
Nigeria

·

THE **DRAGON** IN SHALLOW WATER
BECOMES THE BUTT OF SHRIMPS
China

·

THE **EYES** CLOSE IN SLEEP,
BUT THE PILLOW REMAINS AWAKE
Malaysia

·

IT IS VAIN TO LOOK FOR YESTERDAY'S
FISH IN THE HOUSE OF THE OTTER
India

IF YOU DON'T WANT THE **GUN** TO GO OFF,
DON'T COCK THE TRIGGER
Congo

·

IT TAKES A LONG TIME TO SHARPEN
A **HAMMER** MADE OF WOOD
Holland

·

FOR THE **INVALID**, A DOCTOR;
FOR THE HEALTHY, A SAUSAGE
Estonia

·

TO HIM OF GOOD **JUDGEMENT**, THE SOUND OF
A GNAT SUFFICES; BUT TO HIM WHO LACKS IT,
THE SOUND OF AN ORCHESTRA HELPS HIM NOT
Turkey

·

HE WHO LICKS THE SAUCEPANS AT HOME
WILL NOT BE **KILLED** IN BATTLE
Czech Republic

·

NO MATTER HOW LONG A **LOG** FLOATS ON
THE RIVER, IT WILL NEVER BE A CROCODILE
Mali

BEFORE **MARRYING**, LIVE WILDLY FOR
THREE YEARS
Poland

·

WHEN A PEASANT BECOMES A **NOBLEMAN**,
HE LOOKS AT THE PLOUGH THROUGH SPECTACLES
Germany

·

THOSE WHO DEAL IN **ONIONS**
NO LONGER SMELL THEM
Germany

·

THE STRING OF OUR SACK OF **PATIENCE**
IS GENERALLY TIED WITH A SLIP KNOT
Japan

·

DON'T **QUIT** UNTIL THE HEARSE COMES ROUND
America

·

ALTHOUGH THE **RIVER** IS BROAD,
THERE ARE TIMES WHEN SHIPS COLLIDE
China

·

WHAT'S THE GOOD OF A **SPOON** AFTER
THE MEAL IS OVER?
Latvia

THREE THINGS YOU MUST CROSS THE ROAD
TO AVOID: A FALLING TREE, YOUR BOSS AND
YOUR SECOND WIFE WHISPERING IN AGREEMENT
AND A GOAT WEARING A LEOPARD'S TAIL
China

·

IF YOU **UNDERSTAND** EVERYTHING,
YOU MUST BE MISINFORMED
Japan

·

FROM FOUR THINGS, GOD PRESERVE US:
A PAINTED WOMAN, A CONCEITED **VALET**,
SALT BEEF WITHOUT MUSTARD AND A
LITTLE LATE DINNER
India

·

YOU HAVE NO **WISDOM** IF YOU GO TO SLEEP
BEFORE YOU MAKE YOUR BED
Uganda

·

THE WORK OF THE **YOUTH** IS THE BLANKET
OF THE OLD
Albania

·

ZEAL WITHOUT PRUDENCE IS FRENZY
England

ENGLISH FROM SPANISH AND PORTUGUESE

Armada
Literally, an army. Now, a fleet of armed ships.

[The Spanish Armada was aimed at overthrowing Elizabeth I.
Spain had been angry with the English ever since they began
distancing themselves from the Roman Catholic faith. In 1588,
the King of Spain sent a vast number of ships en route for Britain,
but they were intercepted in the English Channel and were
chased up the eastern coast of England, across the northern coast
of Scotland into the Atlantic and past Ireland. There, severe storms
wrecked more than 24 ships. About a third of the Spanish fleet
failed to return home.]

Bonanza
Literally, prosperity. Used to describe an especially productive
mine. Now, any source of wealth.

Commando
From the Portuguese verb, '*commandar*', to command.
In the plural, a group of armed men formed for a specific
military purpose.

Dodo
Portuguese for 'simpleton'. The dodo was a particularly
useless bird, which did not even taste nice. It has been extinct
since the seventeenth century. Hence, dead as a dodo.

Elixir
Elixir vitae was deemed to be a drug that extended life indefinitely.

Flotilla
The diminutive of '*flota*', a fleet. Now, usually a small number
of warships.

Guacamole

A dish of avocado pears, onions, tomatoes and chili peppers.
An oft-repeated story tells of the sophisticated Lord Mandelson
visiting a chip shop in his constituency of Hartlepool, noticing
what he thought were mushy peas and ordering them as
guacamole. Several years elapsed before Lord Kinnock admitted
having invented the story.

Hacienda

The nearest equivalent is 'smallholding'.

Incommunicado

Out of communication, unable to be contacted.

Junta

Council or committee, but now usually a group of right-wing
army officers running a country after a coup.

Lambada

A fast and erotic dance that originated in Brazil in which the
dancers move in close physical contact with each other. From the
same linguistic origins that give us 'lambast', to beat or to whip.

Manifesto

As a Spanish verb, this means 'to make something clear'.
In English, usually, the policy statement made by a political party
at the start of an election campaign: its authors' stance on a range
of issues is made manifest, clear.

[El] Niño

A shortened form of *El Nino de Navidad*, the Christmas child,
it was originally applied to the natural warming of seawater off
the northern Peruvian coast between Christmas and March
each year. In its more extreme version, it extends across the Pacific
bringing severe change to weather systems.

Oregano
Introduced into English parlance as we became more adventurous in cooking. Akin to 'marjoram', it is another culinary revelation of the past generation or so.

Palaver
The English equivalent of '*palavra*', a Portuguese word meaning 'word' or 'talk'. Through traders in central Africa, it became 'discussions with local chiefs' and then successively 'idle talk' and 'a long, complicated exercise'.

Quinoa
A plant found on the slopes of the Andes and cultivated for its seeds.

Rodeo
The riding of unbroken horses, bucking broncos.

Siesta
The sixth hour, the afternoon nap.

Tequila
A spirit distilled from the sap of a giant cactus.

> ***True story:*** *a reporter was sent to the Canary Islands to cover a health scare affecting British holidaymakers. A Spanish doctor gave him some very good quotes, but refused to be named. The reporter followed him back to his surgery outside which a brass plaque had been fitted bearing the two words he thought he needed. He filed his copy liberally quoting Dr Abierto Domingo. A sub-editor with some knowledge of Spanish put him right.*
> *'Abierto Domingo' means 'Open on Sundays'.*

FIVE QUESTIONS ASKED OF GOOGLE JOB APPLICANTS

1. *How many golf balls can fit into a school bus?*
2. *How much should you charge to wash all the windows in Seattle?*
3. *How many times a day do a clock's hands overlap?*
4. *How many piano tuners are there in the world?*
5. *Why are manhole covers round?*

Members of appointments boards at Goldman Sachs asked interviewees: 'If you were shrunk to the size of a pencil and put in a blender, how would you get out?' Volkswagen asked: 'What would you do if you were to inherit a pizzeria from your uncle?' Employers apparently want candidates to be creative under pressure. There may not even be a correct or incorrect answer. In Google's case, however, there are correct answers:

1. *An algebraic formula is required*
2. *Valhalla, a window-cleaning service in Seattle, supplied a quote: $90 million for all residential windows and $100 million for all those in commercial properties*
3. *Twenty-two*
4. *The Pianoforte Tuners' Association believes there are about 1,000 in Britain. The population of Britain is about 60 million. That is one piano tuner for every 60,000 people. The world population is about 6.75 billion. Extrapolated, that means there would be 111,667 piano tuners in the world if people in other countries were as keen on playing the piano as people in Britain. There are not many pianos outside the Western world, which has a population of 600 million. So, the answer is about 10,000.*
5. *A round cover cannot be dropped down the hole. A square one can.*

WOULD YOU ADAM AND EVE IT?

Have a butcher's at this. Cockney rhyming slang is dying out or so they say. A survey of 2,000 people, half of them from London, found that fewer than 4 per cent knew that 'rabbit and pork' means 'talk'; 6 per cent were aware that 'Vera Lynn' represents gin; and only 8½ per cent knew that 'Cain and Abel' means 'table'.

More understood that 'cream crackered' meant 'knackered', that a 'tea-leaf' was a thief and that 'pork pies' were lies. There must still be a little life left in the patois. The linguistics professor, David Crystal, a much-honoured chronicler of the state of the English language, has heard of people referred to as wearing their 'Barack Obamas', their pyjamas. So, the argot is not quite dead.

However, others say that Cockneys themselves are dying out, if we accept the definition that they must be born within earshot of the bells of St Mary-le-Bow church in Cheapside and not, as is commonly supposed, in the east London district of Bow. That is because London has become so much noisier.

In the middle of the nineteenth century, noise levels were similar to that of the countryside today – roughly 20 to 25 decibels. Now, the area round Cheapside is recording more than 55 decibels. So, whereas previously, the bells could be heard across much of north and east London, they are now picked up only in the City of London and Shoreditch.

Pearly kings and queens are keen to keep the tradition going to the extent that they are giving lessons on the Cockney accent and rhyming slang in the east London borough of Tower Hamlets, in whose schools 126 languages are spoken. They realise, though, that the medium needs to be updated. A 'Ruby Murray', named after the once popular singer, who set the record for having five songs in the Top Twenty at the same time and who later, when arrested

for being drunk, sang the police a medley of her hits from
her cell, used to stand for a curry. Now, it is an Andy Murray
or just an Andy.

Here are some of the people whose names have been
appropriated:

Al Capone .... Phone
Benny Hill ....Drill or till
Calvin Klein .... Fine [or wine]
David Beckham .... Peckham
Emma Freud[s] .... Haemorrhoids
Fatboy Slim .... Gym
Georgio Armani .... Sarnie [sandwich]
Hannibal Lecter .... [Ticket] inspector
Ilie Nastase .... Carsey, karsey, karsy, karzy, kazi
or khazi. Six lavatories.
Jack Dee ....Wee or pee
Ken Dodd[s] .... Cods [testicles]
Lou Reed .... Speed [amphetamines]
Meryl Streep .... Sleep
Nelson Mandela .... Stella [Artois]
Oliver Twist .... Pissed
Posh and Becks ....Sex
Queen Mum ....Bum
Roy Castle .... Arsehole [rather unkind]
Samuel Pepys ....Creeps
Tina Turner .... Learner
Uri Geller ....Another Stella [Artois]
Vincent Price ....Ice
Wallace and Gromit .... Vomit
Yogi Bear .... Chair or lair
Zorba the Greek .... Leak [urinate]

THEIR NAMES LIVE ON

Eponyms: the excellent Guy Keleny pointed out in the
Independent [18 December 2010] that the person who gives
the name is eponymous, but the thing that takes it is not.

Fanny Adams

Aged only eight, Fanny was murdered near her home in
Hampshire in 1867. Her dismembered body was found scattered
over a wide area. Two years later, the Royal Navy introduced
tinned mutton many seamen found inedible. They suggested
that parts of Fanny's body had been discovered at the Navy's
victualling yard in Deptford. 'Sweet Fanny Adams' became slang
for 'mutton' or 'stew', then for anything worthless and finally
for nothing at all, i.e. Sweet F.A. [Fuck All].

Sir John Anderson

As Home Secretary in 1939, Anderson was required to provide
air-raid shelters for people to put up in their back gardens in
preparation for the impending war. Made to the design of the
engineer, William Paterson, about three million shelters were built.

> ***True story:*** *after one air-raid warning, Bill and Vi*
> *fled to their shelter. Halfway there, Vi cried out:*
> *'Bill, I've left my teeth on the draining board.'*
> *Bill's reply: 'For Gawd's sake, woman, they're*
> *throwing bombs, not ham sandwiches.'*

Samuel Benedict

In 1894, Samuel Benedict invented what he thought was the
perfect hangover cure, a breakfast of poached eggs served on
buttered toast and topped with bacon and hollandaise sauce.

Charles Boycott

As an agent for certain estates in County Mayo, Boycott was targeted by the Irish Land League, which tried to shut him off from all commercial and social activities.

Nicolas Chauvin

A soldier in the French Revolutionary Army, he so adored Napoleon that he was widely ridiculed by his comrades. 'Chauvinist' came to be applied to anyone unthinkingly committed to a particular cause.

Draco

As a chief magistrate in Athens in the seventh century BC, he enacted extremely severe laws. From that point on, 'draconian' was applied to any harsh action.

Joseph Guillotin

He proposed to the French assembly that all Frenchmen sentenced to death should be guillotined rather than hanged for humanitarian reasons. The guillotine was used for the first time in 1792. Guillotin himself died peacefully in his own bed of a carbuncle on his shoulder.

Thomas Hobson

He ran a stable in Cambridge and insisted that his customers were offered only the horse that was nearest the stable door. 'Hobson's choice' was therefore no choice at all.

> *Italic type: Invented by the Italian printer, Aldus Manutius, in about 1500. First used in an edition of Virgil's work's in 1501, its new slanting style became known as Italicus, meaning Italian or Italic. [Not really an eponym, but it's interesting, isn't it?]*

Candido Jacuzzi
Invented the whirlpool bath for his son who was born with
rheumatoid arthritis.

Edward Jones
An American statistician, who with Charles Dow helped to found
Dow Jones and Company, a concern remembered now only for
the Dow Jones index, the American equivalent of the Financial
Times index of share prices.

Mikhail Kalashnikov
He invented the widely used assault rifle named after him. It was
first manufactured in 1959. He was honoured in the Soviet Union
as a Hero of Socialist Labour.

Jules Léotard
A French trapeze artist who wore a skintight garment similar
to those used now by dancers and people working out at a gym.
He was honoured in the song, 'The Daring Young Man on the
Flying Trapeze'.

Little Tich
A music-hall comedian who was born Harry Relph. He was
barely four feet tall and anything since regarded as small was often
referred to as 'titchy'.

Marquis de Martinet
Commander of Louis XIV's personal regiment, who gave
his name to a harsh system of drilling young officers. A martinet
[with Anglicised pronunciation] is someone known as a strict
disciplinarian.

Jean Nicot
The French Ambassador to Portugal, introduced tobacco into France. The plant, *Nicotiana* or nicotine, was named after him.

Georg Ohm
Gave his name to the ohm, the unit of electrical resistance.

Vidkun Quisling
A Norwegian politician who betrayed his country to the Germans. Thenceforward, his surname was used to describe anyone who collaborates with the enemy.

Henry Shrapnel
A British artillery officer who invented the Shrapnel shell, which exploded over a wide area, killing or injuring anyone in its path. It was first used widely by Wellington's forces in 1815 and helped to defeat Napoleon at Waterloo.

Ras Tafari
Became Haile Selassie, the emperor of Ethiopia. He was viewed as a hero by some Jamaicans, who called themselves Rastafarians, proud that he had been crowned King of Kings.

Peter Valdo [or Waldo]
Led the Waldensians, who were persecuted as heretical from the twelfth century onwards and were accused of sorcery. French missionaries remembered them when they came across witch doctors preaching black magic in the West Indies. They called them Vaudois, which became corrupted to voodoo.

Count Ferdinand von Zeppelin

After retiring as a lieutenant general at the age of 52, he began
working on the construction of airships. By the turn of the
century, he produced his first dirigible, which was named after
him. The first casualties of an air raid over Britain came when
a Zeppelin dropped bombs on Great Yarmouth in 1915.

Arthur Wellesley, Duke of Wellington

Gave the name of his dukedom to the capital of New Zealand,
a public school and many pubs. But his lasting legacy is a pair
of boots.

Samuel Wilson

Wilson's nickname was Uncle Sam. He was meat packer at Troy
in New York state and during the war of 1812 a government
inspector. He stamped the initials of the United States, which
coincided with those of his nickname, on barrels of meat. In 1813,
the Troy Post printed the first known reference to the American
government as Uncle Sam.

Xenocrates

A pupil of Plato, was a Greek philosopher of strong character
who made up for his relative slowness to learn and his lack
of natural grace by a love of truth and untiring industry.
These characteristics are reflected in the word 'xenocratic'.

Linus Yale

An American locksmith who invented the Yale lock. It was
patented in 1851.

THE COMEDY OF ENGLISH

'Sergeant, arrest most of these vicars' from *See How They Run*, written by Philip King and first staged in Peterborough in 1944. Sir Tom Stoppard commented: 'I wish I'd written that.'

The funniest line in all British drama consists of only two words. In *The Importance of Being Earnest* [1895] by Oscar Wilde, the formidable Lady Bracknell interrogates Jack Worthing, a prospective suitor for her daughter, Gwendolen. She is horrified to learn that he was adopted after being discovered as a baby in a handbag at Victoria Station. Lady Bracknell: 'A handbag?'

I believe the funniest line in television comedy [four words] was heard in *Dad's Army*: 'Don't tell him, Pike!'

German U-boat Captain: *'I am making notes, Captain, and your name will go on the list and, when we win the war, you will be brought to account.'*
Captain Mainwaring: *'You can write what you like. You're not going to win the war.'*
Private Pike: *'[Singing] Whistle while you work. Hitler is a twerp. He's half-barmy. So's his army. Whistle while you work.'*
U-boat Captain: *'Your name will also go on the list! What is it?'*
Mainwaring: *'Don't tell him, Pike!'*

Which all proves that it is not the line that is funny, but the context and the delivery.

The veteran actress, Athene Seyler, had an unusual name that often defied pronunciation [A-thee-knee Sigh-ler]. Once, appearing in a far-flung country, she saw herself billed as 'A Tiny Sailor'.

While several West End theatres were being renamed, the somewhat vain Harold Pinter told Stoppard that he thought the Comedy Theatre should be named after him. Stoppard was unimpressed: 'Wouldn't it be easier if you changed your name to Harold Comedy?' Posthumously, Pinter was granted his wish.

Sir Donald Sinden, a member of the Garrick Club, tells a story about a former distinguished member, Sir Henry Irving, who arrived for dinner one evening and took his seat. A hush fell as those sitting closest to him waited for his first words. 'I was walking with Tennyson in the park this morning,' he said after a long pause. 'A decent fellow, but vain.' Another pause. 'As we walked, people kept raising their hats.' A further pause. 'And he thought it was for him.'

THE LANGUAGE OF FOOD AND WINE

For a long time, it struck many of us as silly that English menus should be printed in French. It was almost as though the food would not be any good if there were not a hint of France about it. Now, of course, eating out in London is far more rewarding than doing so in Paris. The best restaurants in France are outside Paris. But English menus and recipes now have other problems. The first is that the chefs who write menus often use unfathomable language to describe quite ordinary offerings. The second is that some recipes introduce ingredients from all four corners of the planet. So that, on starting to prepare a meal, it is necessary to have not only a cookbook by your side, but several dictionaries, a world gazetteer and the Internet on hand.

Restaurant reviewers have a lot to answer for as well. One, writing for the *Sunday Telegraph*, was enthralled by a duck egg she ate at Sat Bains in Nottingham:

> *Nothing could prepare you for the taste of it.*
> *The albumen, only just opaque, offers a neutral*
> *canvas for flavours I can best describe as ethereal ...*
> *The pea sorbet is beautifully sweet, but self-effacing.*

Some of us, noshing on the lower foothills, have never come across a self-effacing sorbet. Then, there is the recipe for pan-fried scallops with roasted red peppers and marjoram *salmoriglio*. Leaving aside the *salmoriglio*, a southern Italian sauce made of lemon juice, olive oil, garlic, oregano and parsley, and the required splash of Volpaia red wine vinegar for the scallops, the recipe calls for Datterini tomatoes.

Intensive research reveals that the Datterini is a sweet Italian tomato. There are apparently 7, 500 different types of tomato. My greengrocer sells three. Any of them would, I imagine, work here. Another recipe, this one for a salad, demands an amount of mizuna. This is an oriental vegetable, also known as Japanese brassica. I would need to travel to London and scour the capital for mizuna.

A restaurant reviewer refers to chestnut beignets. Turn to the reference books. Beignets are American pastries made from deep-fried dough. There is a starter described as mushrooms on sippets. Should you want to know, sippets are nothing more than toast. The Gilbert Scott restaurant, the brasserie at St Pancras Renaissance Hotel in London, offers duck egg on sippets, as well as soles in coffins, just the snack for a funeral tea.

Even my local restaurant in suddenly chic Leigh-on-Sea offers smoked *pommes aligote* [probably *aligot*], white onion pissaladiére, kune pork sausage, fennel with cavolo nero, mushroom duxelle and sofrito of Provençal.

As for wine writers, well, it appears they absconded to another planet eons ago. One describing a Syrah from the northern Rhone says it 'bursts with gorgeous, inky, oaky yet velvety, bramble and violet-perfumed fruit'. Another French red has 'fat plum, creosote and sandalwood flavours'. Oenophiles must enjoy drinking creosote as a reviewer who had slurped a Spanish red wrote of its 'bold, chocolaty palate and ripe, chunky, creosote-soaked firework finish'. Even Asda does not escape these maniacs' attention. A writer said one of its wines 'reminds me of weathered, lichen-covered, old fence posts'. Wine reviewers must know they are the butt of humour. A Thurber cartoon shows a host telling his guests: 'It's just a naïve domestic Burgundy without any breeding, but I think you'll be amused by its presumption.'

WELL SAID

All my eye and Betty Martin
Meaning 'What nonsense!' A slight variation of the phrase seems to date from the late eighteenth century. On their own, 'my eye' and 'all my eye' go back even further. But who was Betty Martin? She could have been an eighteenth-century actress, but that is just one theory.

Bring on the dancing girls
When P. G. Wodehouse was working on Broadway musicals around 1920, he learned this was a favourite cliché of impresarios. They were really saying 'Let's have something more exciting.'

[I] Close your [my] eyes and think of England
Many sources attribute this quotation to a certain Lady Hillingdon, who is said to have adopted such an attitude when confronted with the awful prospect of having sex with her husband.

Don't do anything I wouldn't do
Dating from about 1910, this gentle warning is in the same league as 'If you can't be good, be careful.' Its first usage is lost in the mists of time. But it has always had a sexual connotation, especially in the Second World War, when addressed to a soldier going on leave for the weekend and expecting it to be a 'dirty' weekend. The usual rejoinder is: 'That gives me plenty of scope.'

Every day and in every way [I'm getting better and better]

A mantra promulgated by a French psychologist, Dr Emile Coué [1857–1926], who believed that his patients could make themselves better through auto-suggestion.

Famous last words

From the 1930s, this was a reply to any such rash statement as, 'It would never happen to me.' In the Second World War, it was a common response in the armed services to an ill-considered statement like 'Flak (bursting artillery shells) is not really dangerous.'

[He's] Gone for a burton

A Second World War RAF euphemism for 'He's missing, presumed dead.' The Burton in question may have been a brewer who produced a beer known in the trade as a 'Burton'.

Home, James, and don't spare the horses

Dating from about 1870, a humorous instruction from a man-about-town to his coachman. In the 1930s, it became the title of a song.

I say, I say, I say

In the archetypal comic music-hall double act, one partner continually interrupted the other with a line such as this. But who said it first? It could have been Murray and Mooney in the 1930s.

Jolly hockey sticks

Slightly poking fun at the hearty gamesmanship prevalent in girls' public schools. Possibly first used as recently as the 1950s by the comedienne, Beryl Reid, playing Monica, the posh girlfriend of Archie Andrews in BBC Radio's *Educating Archie*. Andrews' puppeteer, Peter Brough, was extraordinarily bad. He once asked Beryl: 'Can you see my lips move?' Her reply: 'Only when Archie is talking.'

Keep up with the Joneses

Dripping with social snobbery, this phrase, meaning 'do all you can to match your neighbours', was first seen in 1913 in a comic strip in New York's *The Globe* that used the phrase as its title.

Last of the big-time spenders

Referring to someone who is certainly not. That is to say, someone who spends very little. It may have its origins in the big spenders of the 1920s who had nothing left to spend come the Wall Street crash.

Money talks

The Italian writer, Giovanni Torriano, wrote 'Man prates, but gold speaks.' By the time Wodehouse was writing in 1915, 'Money talks' was certainly in evidence.

Not in front of the children

[or *pas devant les enfants*] originated in Noël Coward's light comedy, *I'll Leave It To You* [1920]: 'Please, not in front of the child.'

On with the motley

In other words, the show must go on, the belief among actors
that any great misfortune must be ignored in the interest of an
audience who have paid to see their show. In the opera, *Pagliacci*
[1892], the main character, Canio, after discovering that his
wife has been unfaithful to him, declaims 'Put on the costume.'
He intends to prepare for his performance as a clown. 'Motley' is
an old English word meaning the clothes of an actor or a clown.

Pardon my French

At one time, anything French was regarded as 'naughty'.
Photographs of bare-breasted girls were marketed as 'Parisian
art studies'. This phrase followed any minor 'bad' language from
one unaccustomed to using it. It dates from the First World War
when British soldiers were, among other things, broadening
their horizons.

Run up the flagpole [and see who salutes]

Let's try the idea and see if it works. From about 1950.

Softly softly catchee monkey

This could probably be defined as 'if you approach a situation
gently, there is more chance of success'. A proverb quoted in 1948
advised 'Softly, softly catch the monkey', which was then given
this more exotic form of words.

That's the way the cookie crumbles

Seems to have originated in the world of American advertising
in about 1950, meaning 'that's the way things are'.

Unlike the home life of our own dear Queen

Apparently, during a production of *Antony and Cleopatra*, Sarah Bernhardt as Cleopatra reacted almost hysterically to the news that Mark Antony had been defeated at the Battle of Actium. In the audience, one British woman turned to her companion and was heard to say 'How very different to the home life of our own dear Queen!'

[And] Very nice too

Dictionaries of quotations date this expression from about 1920. In 1913, however, George Robey recorded a song of this title written by the prolific music-hall composer, Joseph Tabrar.

Warts and all

In an anecdote first noted in 1721, Oliver Cromwell said to an artist about to paint his portrait: 'Remark all these roughnesses, pimples, warts and everything you see. Otherwise, I will never pay a farthing for it.'

[Even] Your best friends won't tell you

From a Listerine mouthwash advert of the 1920s, indicating that halitosis is a taboo subject.

[Feeding time at the] Zoo

Since the 1940s, 'messy eating'. Later, any disorderly scene.

ENGLISH FROM LATIN

Affidavit
Literally, he has sworn. Now, a statement of truth.

Bona fide
[In] Good faith.

Crematorium
A place where corpses are incinerated. [Cosily abbreviated to the crem. A users' guide may describe a five-star award as 'la crème de la crem'.]

Dictum
Originally, merely a saying. Now, a wise saying.

Epitome
Summary of written work. The ancient Greek word, *epitome*, meaning an abridgement, found its way into Latin as *epitoma*.

Forum
Originally, the market place of a Roman town, where presumably important local issues were debated. Now, a discussion group.

Gravitas
Gravity of behaviour or thought.

Hiatus
From '*hiare*', to gape, to stare with an open mouth. So, a gap, a hole.

Impromptu
'*In promptu*', in readiness. So, something spontaneous.

Javelin
Derived from the Latin '*jaculum*' [or '*iaculum*'], a dart.

Limbo
Strictly, the borderland of Hell. So, an intermediate state.

Memento mori
'Remember death', a reminder of immortality.

Non sequitur
'It does not follow'. An abrupt, non–sensical change of subject.

Onomatopoeia
More Greek than Latin; name-making: a word that sounds like an imitation of what it represents, like hiccough, splash and miaow.

Paraphernalia
Originally, the possessions of a wife over which her husband has no control. Now, oddly, bits and pieces. [Another Greek word that found its way into Latin.]

Quorum
'Of them': the minimum number of members of, for example, a committee needed to make decisions.

Rigor mortis
Literally, the stiffness of death. The state of rigidity of the body after death.

Status quo
Literally meaning 'the state in which'. It came to represent 'the situation as it is or was'.

Tempus fugit
Time flies. Virgil wrote '*fugit irreparabile tempus*': time flies irretrievably.

MIND THE GAP

A word of warning – several words, actually: if you ever choose to run your own website, think carefully about the name you pick. When Big Al's bowling alley in Vancouver, Washington State, set one up, it seemed a good idea to call it www.ilovebigals.com, which sounded fine until someone pointed out that read another way it could come out as: I Love Bi Gals. Then, the unwelcome phone calls started.

Similarly, a group of people putting together a list of agents representing famous people called themselves www.whorepresents.com. Wrong again. A team of tree surgeons working in Brittany based their name on the French word for groves or copses, '*bocages*'. Once they were known as www.lesbocages.com, they too attracted unwarranted attention. In New South Wales, there is a gardening company called Mole Station nursery. Their website materialised as www.molestationnursery.com.

An American software designer, Andy Geldman, collects these unfortunate appellations. He found an electricity company with an Italian branch trading under the title www.powergenitalia.com and Pen Island, a company dealing in fountain pens, doing business as www.penisland.net. A high-class outfit, La Drape, concerned with drapes [or curtains] picked the name www.ladrape.com, while a Californian firm listing available therapists started business as www.therapistfinder.com.

A team of computer programmers who exchange advice with each other chose to be known as www.expertsexchange.com. Then, an annual Dutch music festival, Holland's Hit Festival, came on line as www.hollandshitfestival.nl and the Orchestra of the S.E.M. Ensemble, based in New York, reached a wider audience as www.semensemble.org.

AGONY AUNTS

The other day, I set off for work, leaving my recently made-redundant husband in the house watching TV as usual. A hundred yards down the road, my engine conked out and my car juddered to a halt. I walked back home to get my husband's help and found him in the bedroom, dressed in my underwear and high-heeled shoes and wearing my make-up. He broke down and confessed he'd been wearing my clothes for six months. He said he'd begun to feel increasingly depressed after being made redundant from his job. I told him he had to stop or I would leave him. Since this ultimatum, he has become increasingly distant and I don't feel I can get through to him any more. Please can you help?
Mrs B, Essex

Dear Mrs B.
A car stalling after being driven a short distance can be caused by a variety of faults in the engine. Start by checking that there is no debris in the fuel line. Check the jubilee clips holding the vacuum pipes onto the inlet manifold. If none of these approaches solves the problem, it could be the fuel pump itself that is faulty.

TWO LAWS

Murphy's Law states that, if something can go wrong, it will.
Sod's Law states that, if there are two possible results of a situation,
the less favourable will occur.

Much scientific thought has been given as to why, when you
drop a piece of buttered toast, it usually lands on the floor with
the buttered side down. In choosing the word 'usually', scientists
put the likelihood as at least 62 per cent. It is an annoying habit
because, landing buttered side down, the toast is ruined. Any dirt
on the floor is more likely to be absorbed by the butter than
the toast. Scientists explain that, when the toast falls out of your
hand, it is usually at an angle and it then rotates. If you are sitting
at a table or standing up when the accident happens, there is
enough time for the toast to rotate about half a turn and so will
land upside down.

If it is dropped from a height of three metres or more (this applies
to people who eat toast while standing on ladders), there is time
for the toast to rotate a full 360 degrees and land buttered side up.
So the 'buttered toast phenomenon', as it has come to be known,
is an example of both Murphy's Law and Sod's Law.

FAILING POWERS

Auberon Waugh, who suffered from deafness, accepted an
invitation to give a lecture in Africa on breast feeding. He
researched the subject thoroughly and was halfway through
his dissertation when he was stopped. His hosts had expected
him to talk about press freedom.

Late in life, Arthur Marshall was alarmed to hear on the radio
that there had been an armed attack on Debenhams. The target
was, in fact, Lebanon.

SECRET LANGUAGE

Polari is a mongrel language drawn from Italian, Romany and Hebrew. It was used by gay men as a secret code from the mid-nineteenth century until the decriminalisation of homosexuality in 1967. As gay men became more visible from the 1970s onwards, some of the language slipped into the mainstream. Most people became aware of Polari as a result of BBC Radio's *Round the Horne* [1965–8], in which the scriptwriters, Barry Took and Marty Feldman, cast Hugh Paddick and Kenneth Williams as two outrageous gay men, Julian and Sandy. This was dangerous comedy. When the show began, men could be sent to prison for homosexual acts. The sketches always featured the ultra-straight star of the show, Kenneth Horne, who was oblivious [or perhaps ignorant or merely playing along] of the camp patois and double entendres emanating from Julian and Sandy. On one occasion, Sandy disclosed that Julian had been swept overboard while sailing round the world:

Horne: *But did you manage to drag yourself up on deck?*
Julian: *Ooh, no, we dressed quite casual.*

Another example:

Sandy: *Don't mention Malaga to Julian. He got very badly stung.*
Horne: *Portuguese man o' war?*
Julian: *Well, I never saw him in uniform…*

TWO VERSIONS OF THE LORD'S PRAYER

1. Twenty-first century English

Our universal chairperson in Outer Space,
Your identity enjoys the highest rating on a prioritised selectivity scale.
May your sphere of influence take on reality parameters.
May your mindset be implemented on this planet as in Outer Space.
Allot to us at this point in time and on a per diem basis
A sufficient and balanced dietary food intake
And rationalise a disclaimer against our negative feedback
As we rationalise a disclaimer against the negative feedback of others.
And de-programme our negative potentialities
But desensitise the impact of the counter-productive force.
For yours is the dominant sphere of influence,
The ultimate capability and the highest qualitative analysis rating
At this point in time and extending beyond a limited time-frame.
End of message.

2. For travellers round London

Our Farnham, which art in Hendon,
Harrow be thy name.
Thy Kingston come, thy Wimbledon
In Erith as it is in Hendon.
Give us this day our Leatherhead.
Forgive us our by-passes and
Lead us not into Thames Ditton
But deliver us from Esher.
For thine is the Kingston,
The Purley and the Crawley.
For Esher and Esher
Crouch End.

DON'T BELIEVE EVERYTHING YOU READ

Hoaxers are to be found in all types of people, even academics, who, you might think, would neither have the time nor the sense of humour to go to all the trouble.

The German-language *Der Neue Pauly. Enzyklopädie der Antike* includes a deadpan description of a fictional Roman sport, *apopudobalia,* which appears to resemble modern soccer.

The 1975 *New Columbia Encyclopedia* contains an entry on one Lillian Virginia Mountweazel [1942-1973]. She was said to have been a fountain designer and photographer, best known for her collection of photos of rural American letterboxes. She reputedly died in an explosion while on an assignment for the magazine, *Combustibles.*

The first printing of the 1980 *New Grove Dictionary of Music and Musicians* carries an entry for a nineteenth-century Danish flautist, conductor and composer, Dag Henrik Esrum-Hellerup. His opera, *Alys og Elvertoj* [now lost], was said to be much admired by Smetana. Bibliography: A. Pirro: *Esrum-Hellerup: Sa Vie and Son Oeuvre* [Paris, 1919]. The spoofer was the musicologist, Robert Layton.

NEW TO ME

The *Oxford English Dictionary* dredges newspapers for the first-known use of a word. *The Times* and the *Daily Telegraph* frequently prove useful:

1820 pianist *The Times*	**1864** extradite *Daily Telegraph*
1820 paprika *The Times*	**1865** extremism *Daily Telegraph*
1839 pre-paid *The Times*	**1887** underdog *Daily Telegraph*

A study of more recent history provides the year in which a word or phrase was used for the first time. The concept may have existed beforehand, but the word was not coined until the year shown alongside it. There is a touch here of social history in microcosm:

1900
coitus interruptus;
heterosexuality;
voyeur

1901
bird-watching;
concentration
camp;
executive;
flyover;
weekend

1902
birthday card;
cakewalk;
chauffeur;
floosie/floozie;
garage;
matinee idol

1903
clone

1904
hangover

1905
colour prejudice

1906
conveyor belt;
paedophilia

1907
anorexic;
bath salts;
Rottweiler;
television

1908
Tin Pan Alley

1909
brassiere;
jazz;
jigsaw;
libido

1910
avant-garde;
double-glazed;
moron;
taramasalata

1911
sex symbol;
vamp

1912
blues;
homosexual;
schizophrenia;
vitamin

1913
anti-freeze;
massage parlour;
talkie

1914
shish kebab

1916
back–packing;
footage

1917
traffic jam

1918
climax [sexually];
lounge lizard;
posh

1919
jamboree

1920
bathing beauty;
comic strip;
deflation;
gold digger;
T-shirt;
wimp

1922
fascism;
transvestite

1923
council house;
hi–jack;
hitch–hike;
robot

1924
face-lifting;
photocopy

1925
blind date;
crazy paving;
lesbian;
newsreader

1926
by–pass;
car park;
re–cycle;
sugar daddy

1927
myxomatosis;
tap dancer;
zip fastener

1928
cocktail party

1929
astronaut;
crisps;
football pools;
greenhouse
effect;
traffic light

1930
air-conditioning;
burger;
jingle;
negligee;
scampi

1931
barbecue;
black market;

1932
Aryan;
green belt;
yo-yo

1933
supermarket

1935
milk bar;
pizza;
video

1936
bingo;
house arrest;
parking meter;
strip tease

1937
logo

1938
muzak;
payola

1939
juke box;
muesli;
rat race;
soap opera

1940
counselling;
crew-cut;
holiday camp

1941
disc jockey;
gremlin;
jeep;
moussaka;
pin-up;
quiz

1942
napalm;
organic

1943
red-brick

1944
anti-biotic;
gobbledygook;
vegan

1945
computer;
espresso

1947
apartheid

1948
fax

1949
cortisone;
launderette;
Sellotape;
supercalifragilistic
expialidocious

1950
ayatollah;
brainwashing;
eiderdown;
hi-fi;
zebra crossing

1951
fast food;
garlic bread

1952
credit card;
do-it-yourself;
hallucinogenic

1953
boutique;
hippie;
snorkel;
stiletto heel;
videotape;
Y-fronts

1954
discotheque;
rock 'n' roll

1955
bouffant;
karate

1956
brinkmanship;
jeans

1957
candy floss;
felt-tip pen;
Hell's Angel

1958
doner kebab;
modem;
sliced bread;
tandoori;
thalidomide;
transistor radio

1959
charisma;
fabulous;
hair spray;
traffic warden

1960
cassette;
theme park

1962
glitch

1963
bar code;
brain drain;
pantyhose

1964
chicken kiev;
prime time;
water cannon

1965
cable television;
computer game;
freak out;
garden centre;
microwave;
mobile phone;
street-wise

1966
kung-fu;
satellite television

1967
groupie

1968
black hole;
unisex

1969
chat show;
juggernaut

1970
jobsworth;
male chauvinism;
politically correct

1971
passive smoking

1972
bag lady

1973
junk food;
tug-of-love

1974
food processor

1975
debit card;
drive time

1976
bulimia

1977
bottle bank;
e number

1979
compact disc;
karaoke

1980
alternative comedy;
mountain bike;
power dressing;
sound bite;
voice mail;
wheel clamp

1981
gridlock;
stripagram;
toy boy;
wine bar

1982
break dancing;
camcorder;
cyberspace;
scratch card;
spread sheet;
zero tolerance

1983
bog standard;
hacker;
repetitive strain
injury;
safe pair of hands

1984
anorak
*[someone obsessively
interested in an obscure
interest, such as train-
spotting. Such a person
may wear an anorak
because it is cheap
and has many pockets
in which notebooks and
pencils can be kept];*
spin doctor;
wheelie bin;
yuppie

1985
car boot sale;
ciabatta;
cutting edge;
Prozac

1986
bouncy castle;
Internet

1987
champagne
socialist;
lager lout

1988
lap dancing;
pot noodle;
road rage

1989
feeding frenzy

1990
Essex man;
happy clappy;
luvvie

1991
bad hair day;
dumb down;
Essex girl

1992
negative equity;
saddo

1993
off message

1994
clear blue water;
cyber café;
DVD;
spam;
website

1995
alcopop

1998
Viagra

1999
google *[as a verb]*

2000
bling bling
*[ostentatious
jewellery]*

2001
9/11
*[a form of shorthand
for the al-Qaeda
attacks on New York
on 11 September
2001]*

2002
SARS,
*[an acronym forsevere
acute respiratory
syndrome, which in
one pandemic
between November
2002 and July
2003 killed nearly
800 people]*

2003
sex up
*[to make more
interesting as in the
notorious Iraq war
dossier]*

2004
chav
*[a working-class
teenager repeatedly
engaged in anti-
social behaviour]*

2005
sudoku
[a numbers puzzle]

2006
WAGs
*[an acronym used
by tabloid
newspapers to
describe the wives
and girlfriends
of well-known
football players]*

2007
carbon foot–
print
*[a measure of the
impact our activities
have on the
environment,
particularly climate
change]*

2008
Facebook

2009
staycation
*[when the world
recession began to
bite, the media made
up this word to
describe a holiday at
home for people who
could no longer afford
to go abroad]*

2010
vuvuzela
*[a horn sounded at
football matches in
South Africa and
heard around the
world when South
Africa hosted the
FIFA World Cup]*

2011
Man 'flu
*A cold suffered by
a man feeling sorry
for himself.*

2012
chillaxing
*[another
portmanteau word:
a hybrid of 'chilling
out' and 'relaxing']*

2013
tombstoning
*[diving from a high
cliff into water whose
depth has not been
determined]*

PUNCTUATION *IS* IMPORTANT

One letter, two different sets of punctuation:

Dear Jack,
I want a man who knows what love is all about. You are generous, kind, thoughtful. People who are not like you admit to being useless and inferior. You have ruined me for other men. I yearn for you. I have no feelings whatsoever when we're apart. I can be forever happy. Will you let me be yours?
Jill

Dear Jack,
I want a man who knows what love is. All about you are generous, kind, thoughtful people, who are not like you. Admit to being useless and inferior. You have ruined me. For other men, I yearn. For you, I have no feelings whatsoever. When we're apart, I can be forever happy. Will you let me be?
Yours,
Jill

Lynne Truss, who wrote *Eats, Shoots and Leaves*, the best-selling book about punctuation, said: 'I thought the only type of writing guaranteed to make money is in ransom notes. But, oddly enough, I have changed my opinion.'

SEVEN OBITUARIES

G. K. Chesterton once said that 'journalism largely consists
of saying "Lord Jones is dead" to people who never knew that
Lord Jones was alive in the first place.' That is certainly true
of gossip columns in which the behaviour of some minor
actors and models is reported so frequently that they become
famous through sheer repetition. Obituaries have an appeal all
of their own:

Fred Atkins *[1914–83]*
Recognised as a world authority on mushrooms, he travelled
extensively giving lectures and wrote several authoritative works
on the subject, including *Mushroom Growing Today*. He was
a founder member of the Mushroom Growers' Association of
Great Britain and Northern Ireland and in 1955 he was elected
honorary president of the third International Conference on
Mushroom Science, which was held in Paris. In 1966, he was
awarded an OBE for his services to mushroom growing and in
1970 he was made a Knight of the National Order of Agricultural
Merit by the French government.

Santos Casani *[1898–1983]*
He was a leading teacher of ballroom dancing before the Second
World War and later developed a system of rehabilitation for
disabled servicemen. As a member of the Royal Flying Corps
during the First World War, he underwent 27 operations after
crashing in France and receiving terrible burns. He was
discharged from hospital in 1921 with an artificial nose and
a determination to become the world's greatest exponent of
fashionable new dances. In the Second World War, he received
spinal injuries that ended his dancing career. His wife, whom
he married in 1951, had lost a leg in a wartime raid on Cardiff.
He met her at a party for limbless people and eventually taught
her to dance.

Joyce Jillson *[1945–2004]*

Jillson was the official astrologer of Twentieth Century Fox, who consulted her on when to release their films. She was asked to select a date in 1977 for the first Star Wars movie. Given that it became the second biggest grossing movie of all time, she was able to claim success. Other clients included the Ford Motor Company, who paid her to tell them when to launch a new model. She also claimed to have advised Ronald Reagan on who to choose as his running mate in the 1980 presidential election: Senator George H.W. Bush. By the end of her life, her horoscope column, which was syndicated in 314 newspapers around the world, was read by 40 million people. Her prediction for her fellow Capricorns on the day she died was: 'You're bound to have a good time and meet interesting people.'

Earl Russell *[1921–87]*

The son of the philosopher, Bertrand Russell, the fourth Earl Russell occasionally startled his fellow peers in the House of Lords with controversial speeches. During one debate, he advocated the abolition of law and order while insisting that the police should be prevented from raping youngsters in their cells. He had other plans just for girls, recommending that by the time they reached twelve, they should be given a home of their own. In addition, the marriage laws should be anulled so that a girl could have as many husbands as she wanted. Earl Russell's mother, with whom he lived in a dilapidated cottage near Land's End, helped to publish his speech, describing him as the first man since Guy Fawkes to enter the Houses of Parliament with an honest intention. He died while on a train to Penzance.

Sir Melford Stevenson *[1902–87]*

An Old Bailey judge, Sir Melford Stevenson was known for his trenchant views. In a reference to a man in a court case, he said: 'He chose to live in Manchester, a wholly incomprehensible choice for any free man to make.' Once, Stevenson presided over a murder trial involving the Kray brothers. In his view, the gangsters told the truth only twice during the course of proceedings, once when one of the brothers described his barrister as a fat slob, secondly when the other brother claimed the judge was biased. After retiring, Stevenson was asked if he had ever been hurt by criticisms made of him during his career. His response: 'A lot of my colleagues are just constipated Methodists.'

Sir Rex Surridge [1899–1990]
The former acting governor of Tanganyika; he campaigned hard in the 1940s against a government scheme to plant ground-nuts in the country's rocky wilderness. At Oxford, Surridge founded the Venetian Blinds Club, whose members debagged undergraduates who failed to stand for grace or the loyal toast. One night, two members lit bundles of faggots under the front door of the President of St John's College, who had banned the club. To help prepare the ground-nuts scheme, enormous tractors cleared the bush. On one occasion, a convoy of 100-ton railway trucks arrived with bags thought to contain fertiliser. When it was spread over the land, it was found to be cement. There was no suggestion that Sir Rex was associated with such an unfortunate mishap.

Mario Zacchini [1910–98]
The last surviving member of an original generation of human cannonballs. He was one of seven sons of Ildebrando Zacchini, a gymnast who created the Circus Olympia in Italy in the early 1900s. In time, five of the brothers flew from a cannon usually at 90 mph. 'Flying isn't the hard part,' Mario once said. 'Landing in the net is.'

A circus owner, on being told that his human cannonball had died, paid tribute:
'This is a sad loss.
Men of his calibre are hard to find.'

FAMOUS LAST WORDS

François Rabelais, French humorist *[1494–1553]:*
Bring down the curtain, the farce is over

Madame Rolland, French authoress *[1866–1944]:*
O! Liberty, what crimes are committed in thy name

Elvis Presley, Entertainer *[1935–77]:*
Honey, I'm going to take a shit

BIBLIOGRAPHY

Abbott, Geoffrey
The Who's Who of British Beheadings
Andre Deutsch Ltd, 2000

Anon
Weymouth, the English Naples
Hood and Company, 1910

Baldwin, Edward A. and Steve
The Great Pantyhose Crafts Book
Western Publishing Company, 1982

Benson, Ragnar
Gun-Running for Fun and Profit
Paladin Press, 1986

Hirschfeld, Isador
The Toothbrush: Its Use and Abuse
Dental Items of Interest Publishing Company, 1939

Hunting, Anthony L.L.
Encyclopedia of Shampoo Ingredients
Cranford, 1983

Kriwaczek, Rohan
An Incomplete History of the Art of Funerary Violin
Overlook Press, 2006

Mitchell, Tim and Penzer, Rebecca
Psoriasis at Your Fingertips
Class Publishing, 2000

Montague, Julian
The Stray Shopping Carts of Eastern North America
Harry N. Abrams, 2006

Roberts, Wess
Leadership Secrets of Attila the Hun
Bantam Books, 1989

Trimmer, John W.
How to Avoid Huge Ships
Cornell Maritime Press, 1993

Walton, Frederick
The Infancy and Development of Linoleum Floorcloth
Simpkin, Marshall, Hamilton, 1925

Woodall, Allen and Brickell, Sean
The Illustrated Encyclopedia of Metal Lunch Boxes
Schiffer Publications, 1997

POSTSCRIPT

Anyone preaching about the proper use of English is a sitting
target [cliché]. Some of you may have found errors in these pages.
Alistair Cooke said that every book contained at least one mistake.
But, if you have found any here, please do not tell me. I would
only be upset. Or I would be only upset.

ACKNOWLEDGEMENTS

My thanks to Scott Solder, the former editor of BBC Radio 5 live's award-winning breakfast show, who was kind enough to proofread this mishmash, and to Ryan Edwards, who, understanding all the technology now required to produce a workable manuscript, gave freely of his expertise.